W9-APH-760

Praise for *Sky*

"Readers will find themselves caught up in the author's story, rooting for her survival."
—*The Horn Book Magazine*

"Thrilling, informative, and very readable."
—*Children's Book Review Service*

"An involving account . . . This re-creation of one person's experiences can become an extraordinary experience for countless young readers."
—*Bulletin of the Center for Children's Books*

A *Bulletin of the Center for Children's Books*
Blue Ribbon Book
★
A CBC/NCSS Notable Children's Trade Book
in the Field of Social Studies
★
New York Public Library 1997 Books for the
Teen Age

FOR DAVID!

Hanneke Ippisch

LET US REMEMBER......

Photo on facing page: Sailing with friends, 1940. I am to the far right. (Courtesy of the author)

SKY

*A TRUE STORY OF COURAGE
DURING WORLD WAR II*

*illustrated with photographs, documents,
and letters from the author's collection*

HANNEKE IPPISCH

I am now seventy, and I cannot find the excuses to postpone this any longer. At least the grandchildren and our young friends will know what happened so many years ago, and perhaps they will learn from it and understand how life was when I was a child, as they are now. So here it is: for the grandchildren, Annie and Erika, little Natalie and Olivia Rose, and for our friends Shea and Kwaku.

Copyright © 1996 by Hanneke Ippisch.

Published by Troll Communications L.L.C.

All rights reserved. No part of this book may be reproduced or utilized in any form or by any me&
electronic or mechanical, including photocopying, recording, or by any information storage and ret&
system, without written permission from the publisher.

This edition is reprinted by arrangement with Simon & Schuster Children's Publishing Divisio&
First paperback edition 1998.

Book design by Heather Wood.
Map by Claudia Carlson.
Cover design by Shi Chen.

PRINTED IN CANADA
10 9 8 7 6

This edition published in 2003
Library of Congress Cataloging-in-Publication Data
Ippisch, Hanneke.
Sky:{a true story of courage during World War II} / by Hanneke Ippisch.
p.   cm.   Includes index.
Summary: The true story of a young girl's involvement with the Dutch Resistance during World W&
and her subsequent arrest and imprisonment by the Germans.
ISBN 0-689-80508-X (lib. bdg.), ISBN 0-8167-4524-2 (pbk.)
1. Ippisch, Hanneke—Juvenile literature.
2. World War, 1939-1945—Underground movements—Netherlands—Juvenile literature.
3. World War, 1939-1945—Personal narratives, Dutch—Juvenile literature. 4. World War, 19&
1945—Prisoners and prisons, German—Juvenile literature. 5. World War, 1939-1945—Childre&
Netherlands—Juvenile literature. 6. Prisoners of War—Netherlands—Juvenile literature. 7.Yout&
Netherlands—Biography—Juvenile literature.
{1. Ippisch, Hanneke. 2. World War, 1939-1945—Underground movements—Netherlands.
3. Prisoners of war. 4. Netherlands—History—German occupation, 1940-1945.} I. Title.
D802.N4I66   1996   940.53'492'092'—dc20   {B}   95-44065

Contents

Prologue

FACES

I remember many faces, young ones and old, white faces with large worried eyes. I remember that sometimes there were tears in those eyes and the mouths were trembling. I remember a shy smile on some of those faces, but never a broad, happy smile. I remember shadows of people hiding in corners and in attics and underneath floors. The faces I remember belonged to those shadows, many rows of shadows, silent and bent down. I remember when those shadows with the white faces and worried eyes were sent to the east in long trains, heavily guarded.

I remember the whistle of the locomotive pulling those long trains through the Dutch countryside. And those of us who listened to the sound of the whistle knew it was the cry of the thousands going by on their way to the east, on their way to their end.

I knew so few of the names belonging to those faces, waves upon waves of faces going by.

1

The Zeppelin, Holland, 1929

It was a very quiet day, when there were no clouds in the sky, when there was no wind, and the only sounds I heard were the occasional mooing of a cow far away and the chirping of a cricket in the grass near my small feet. I was four years old.

I looked up at the sky. High above me something huge and gray and silent floated slowly, very slowly through the blue heavens. I stared and marveled, and I longed to be up there with it. I was not aware that this floating thing in the sky was the pride of the German nation, the famous zeppelin *Hindenburg*[1] on its maiden voyage, the same zeppelin that some years later would come to a horrible end, burning and crashing so nothing was left.

2

THE FIRST SCHOOL DAY

My first day in school, 1930. My sister is to the right, and I am to the left. I am proudly holding my branch from the old tree. (Photograph by Jan Eikema)

In our village, starting school was a great and wondrous event. You see, we were told that in the dark attic of the village school a tree grew—an old and gnarled tree—and from its branches raisin buns and small white sacks full of hard lemon candy sprouted. And on the very first day of school each new child received a branch laden with buns and candy.

In Holland stands a house.
In Holland stands a house.
Heigh-o jog jiggety, ting-a-ling,
Join hands together and form a ring,
In Holland stands a house.

And in it lives a man,
The man he has a wife,
The wife she has a child,
The child it has a maid,
The maid she has a boy,
The boy he has a dog,
The maid she has a cat.

Now the dog turns out the cat,
And the boy turns out the dog,
And the maid sends off the boy,
And the wife sends off the maid,
And the wife now leaves the house,
And the man must leave it, too,
And the house now catches fire,
And the child is left alone.[2]

3
MY MOTHER

My mother, sister, and me in 1928. I am sitting to the left. My mother is cleaning the butter from the paper. (Photograph by Jan Eikema)

My mother was very serious and quite strict. She taught business, shorthand, bookkeeping, and related subjects, which was rather unusual for women in the early 1900s. She was also frugal and she always managed to save money to buy incredibly beautiful old Dutch antiques. She was so frugal that when she took the paper off a cube of butter, she always scraped the paper clean with a knife, to salvage the last small residue of the butter.

My mother was quite advanced for her time: One day we had a parade in our town. My mother and father spent long hours building a cover on our beach cart so that it looked like a miniature covered wagon. Then they decorated it completely with red dahlias. Mother had our seamstress sew red cotton knit slacks with bibs and suspenders for my sister and me, and we pulled the decorated beach cart in the parade, very proud in our lovely outfits. We won first prize and were very excited to each receive a pewter vase.

The whole town talked about this: "The minister's daughters wearing pants!!!" Some folks totally disapproved and others, I think, were envious that they had not performed this daring feat of dressing their daughters in something so unusual as pants.

My sister (left) and me (right) wearing our red pants and pulling our cart in the parade, 1933. Our signs read Wie gaat mee naar Schagen aan zee *("Who comes along to Schagen at the sea"). (Photograph by Jan Eikema)*

4

THE DOORBELL

My father and mother in 1935. (Courtesy of the author)

I grew up in a busy household. My mother was always occupied keeping the home running smoothly, and my father was working very hard to be a good minister. My sister, two years older than I, busied herself with her hobbies and her schoolwork.

We did not have any chores, because when we were young, ministers' families were rather well-off. There was always a maid to do all the housework and the cooking, and a gardener to take care of the outside. I would watch the gardener wash the windows, and I watched him polish the brass doorbell until it was so shiny, I could see in it the reflections of the sun and the sky.

That nicely polished doorbell rang constantly in the

mornings. The members of my father's church who owned businesses in our town were pleased to have the minister and his family as their customers. Everyone took turns delivering things.

The parsonage—our home—in Godlinze, northeast Holland (close to the German border), 1929. (Courtesy of the author)

One baker delivered white bread every other day, and another baker brought brown bread, and still another one delivered small dark rye bread every third day. There were two milkmen who came with their carts and horses. They also took turns. On Mondays, one liter of milk and one liter of buttermilk were brought by one milkman, on Tuesdays one dozen eggs were brought from the other, and on and on it went.

The greengrocer rang the doorbell every day to ask what kind of fresh vegetables we wanted for dinner. Every Friday morning the flower vendor showed up with his cart full of fresh flowers, and the coal man delivered a sack of coal every week in the wintertime.

There was the butcher riding his bicycle with a large square wicker basket attached to the handlebars, full of meats and sausages; and the *voddenman* ("rag man") who hollered loudly through the streets, *"vodden, mooie vodden"* ("rags, beautiful rags"), while pushing his cart in front of him.

Then, of course, there

My sister, our maid, and me in Godlinze, 1930. I am standing. (Photograph by Jan Eikema)

My sister (left) and me (right), 1936.
(Photograph by Jan Eikema)

Our gardener. (Courtesy of the author)

were all the visitors who wanted to see the *dominee* ("minister") to talk about weddings, baptisms, funerals, or nothing in particular. I often tried to listen, from behind the door of my father's study, to the conversations between my father and a visitor. Mostly I did not grasp what they were talking about, but still, I found it very interesting and exciting.

One day my father caught me eavesdropping. He was very angry and to punish me he put me in a small room with a little window and locked the door. He forgot about me, and after a long time I opened the window and climbed out. It was a *very* long time before I ever listened from behind the door of my father's study again.

But the doorbell rang constantly in the morning on weekdays, and the clear sound was like music vibrating through the air and reaching for the high blue sky.

5

THE LONGBOATS

There are three large rivers flowing from the east through the flat lands of Holland until they reach the North Sea. They are the Rhine, the Waal, and the Maas. The large rivers connect with smaller rivers and with the canals, which crisscross the land as if drawn upon it with pencil and ruler. On those rivers navigate endless rows of long flat boats called *Aken*.[3]

Aken *navigating the river Waal in 1986, when I revisited the Netherlands with my husband. Scenes such as this look much the same as they did in the 1930s and 1940s. (Photograph by Jan Meyer)*

Exploring the Dutch canals in my kayak, 1940. (Photograph by Miep de Wit)

In 1938, when I belonged to a Girl Scout troop in northern Holland, we often went kayaking on the canals and the smaller rivers. I would sit on top of one of the many dikes flanking the waterways and watch the steady traffic going up and down the river. Some of the longboats were lying low, their loads heavy, and you could barely see the top of the cargo. Only the captain's bridge showed high above the water, with the red, white, and blue Dutch flag blowing in the wind behind the bridge. The small windows of the family's living quarters were framed with starched white lace curtains. Potted geraniums bloomed bright red.

Other boats were empty and riding high above the water on their way to Rotterdam to load new cargo. Hundred-meter longboats loaded with huge amounts of coal looked like floating black mountains. Not a minute went by without a boat or two passing. Endless rows of longboats—silent but steady, sliding by. I wanted to live on such a boat, to belong to a skipper's family, to be on a river, and to travel from country to country.

On Sundays not many boats moved. The families who owned and lived on the longboats anchored. The school-age children spent the week in a special, centrally located "skipper's school" (a boarding school for skipper's children) and went home to the longboats on the weekends to be with their parents.

The whole family would ride their bicycles to church. After the sermon they often toured the countryside and then went back to their longboat for supper. In the coldest winters, when ice froze the canals and rivers, the boats stayed anchored for longer periods. Then the skipper's family put on their skates and I would watch them skating, one behind the other, against the ever-blowing wind.

A horse pulling a longboat. The man leading the horse is called the "hunter." (Courtesy of the author)

6

MY FIRST LOVE

Every morning when it was time to walk the one and a half miles to school, where I was finishing eighth grade, a boy was waiting outside of my home with his bicycle. It was Teun, my boyfriend. He had flaxen hair and a red face.

"Good morning," he said. "Good morning," I said. And then we walked together, not saying anything, and he was holding his bike. When we reached the school he said, "I will see you at lunchtime." And I answered, "Okay," and we parted, each to our own classes.

At noon when I was to walk home for lunch, there was Teun, with his bicycle. We walked quietly and when we arrived at my house he said, "See you soon." And I answered, "All right." He jumped on his bike and rode to his home, about two miles from mine.

Half an hour later, ready to go back to school after lunch at my home, there was Teun, bicycle in hand, waiting for me.

Classmates in my Zaandam school, 1938. I am in the first row, third from the left. (Courtesy of the author)

"Hello," he said when I came out of my house. "Hi," I answered. And we walked together back to the high school, where we parted.

When school was out at 4:15 P.M., Teun was there waiting for me, with his bike. "Much homework?" he asked. "Yes," I said, "lots." And we walked together back to my house, he walking his bike. When we came to my house he said, "Good-bye, have a good evening." And I answered, "Thank you, the same to you." And he jumped on his bike and pedaled away.

This daily routine went on for many months, seven to be exact. We talked a little more each day, but not much more.

Then the day arrived when he asked me to go with him to a dance! I accepted and wore my prettiest skirt and blouse, with kneesocks, and my Girl Scout hiking boots because I thought we were going to walk to the dance—five miles away. Besides, I did not have hose and fancy shoes.

When Teun arrived at my house on his bicycle, all

handsome-looking in a white shirt with a tie and dark pants and shiny black shoes, he handed me three daisies he had picked. I blushed and pinned them on my blouse.

"Okay," he said, "get on." So I sat myself behind him on the little luggage carrier of his bike, feet dragging on the ground. That's how we went together on my first date to my first dance.

7

THE WAR BEGINS, MAY 10, 1940

BY THE BEGINNING OF 1940 MOST EUROPEAN COUNTRIES HAD
BEEN TOUCHED BY WAR. THE GERMAN ARMY HAD INVADED AND
OCCUPIED FRANCE, BELGIUM, NORWAY, AND DENMARK. FOR A
SHORT TIME HOLLAND REMAINED INDEPENDENT AND AT PEACE.
BECAUSE OF THE GREAT SECRECY IMPOSED BY THE OCCUPYING
GERMANS, THE REST OF THE WORLD, INCLUDING MOST OF THE
DUTCH PEOPLE, REMAINED UNAWARE OF ALL THE HAPPENINGS IN
THE OCCUPIED LANDS. THE DUTCH COULD NOT BELIEVE ANY-
THING COULD HAPPEN TO THEIR SMALL, BUT FIERCELY INDEPEN-
DENT COUNTRY.

It was one of those soft mornings in early May, when the sun came
up smiling. All was quiet and everybody was fast asleep. I was
dreaming of Girl Scout camps and long trips in my kayak, exploring the many small canals crossing the flat lands of North
Holland.

We woke up suddenly, the whole family. The morning was not quiet anymore: The drone of heavy airplanes flying

overhead filled our ears. My father and mother ran out of their bed-room, and my sister and I ran downstairs and joined them in the kitchen. We looked at each other with amazement, not knowing why so many planes were flying so very low over our heads, barely missing the rooftops. All of us went to the windows and looked out. My father turned on the radio and we heard: "HOLLAND is at war! The German nation is trying to occupy Holland, but the Dutch Army is fighting bravely and is preventing the enemy from gaining much territory." We rushed outside and what we saw was beyond anything we could have imagined: It seemed to be snow-ing giant snowflakes out of the clear blue sky, but we realized the snowflakes were white parachutes carrying German soldiers. Thou-sands upon thousands floated slowly down and landed in our coun-try.

Not knowing what to do, we went inside and listened to the radio again. By this time instructions were being given to the Dutch people: We were told to tape our windows up and down and across so that only small portions of clear glass would show. Then the window glass would not shatter when bombs, possibly close by, exploded. We were told to stay inside as much as possi-ble, and not to panic. Schools and offices would be closed.

My sister was quickly sent to the store to buy six rolls of masking tape and when she returned, we started to tape win-dows. We listened to the radio and I peeked through the untaped squares in the windows to see if the enemy was coming. I was excited; it seemed to be such a big adventure. We heard the con-stant drone of many, many planes, the occasional explosions of bombs far away, and the sound of machine guns in the distance.

When nightfall came, all the people gathered in the streets to talk and to find out if there was any news. I ran from one group of neighbors to the other to listen to what they had heard and reported back to my parents. My father tried to calm some of the folks who were crying.

Rumors ran rampant. It was said that many of the Dutch ammunition boxes, when opened by the Dutch soldiers, were found to be sabotaged—full of sand instead of ammo. It was also said that the battle against the enemy could not last long. But heavy fighting broke out in the central part of Holland, close to the towns of Rhenen and Wageningen, along the river Rhine. Many people living there were ordered by the Civil Service to evacuate.

During the three-day war my family and all others in our town stayed mostly inside and listened to the radio. On the second day, May 11, we heard, "The Dutch soldiers are fighting valiantly. They know it is hopeless, yet they fight. The Dutch government asks everyone to stay in their homes, remain calm, and listen to reports of developments."

On the third day we heard, "The Dutch Army has surrendered. There were too few against so very many. The royal family traveled during the night to England together with some members of the Dutch government. They plan to organize a temporary government in London and . . . this is the end of our program. May God be with you."

The Occupational Forces entered Holland. They looked old, weary, and shabby in their faded green uniforms. Some rode bicycles; many marched. Some Dutchmen looked; many turned their backs. My father told my sister and me to stay inside. My mother, who had not felt well for quite some time, was in bed. Our town had been spared from fighting and from bombing, and our house, as the other houses in Zaandam, was not damaged. Three hundred Dutchmen committed suicide after the surrender. It was the beginning of a new, threatening life for us all.

8

A GIRL SCOUT CAMP

The Dutch Red Cross wanted to have as much donated blood as possible for the wounded soldiers. Our Girl Scout troop was directed to ring doorbells to ask the people to donate blood. We spent two days doing this, and I felt very important to be able to help in this way. Because the fighting did not last long, the Dutch Red Cross had lots of blood.

Boat race on one of Holland's canals in 1940. I am the helmswoman facing the oarswomen in the last seat of the near boat. We won the national championship in this class. (Courtesy of the author)

After the Germans occupied Holland, we continued having our Girl Scout meetings, which took much of our time. Every effort was made by all to carry on a normal life.

We had great programs in our clubhouse, which was in an old windmill called *Het jonge schaap* ("The Young Sheep"). All windmills in Holland had names. We kept rowboats and kayaks in this windmill and made many trips in our small boats. We learned navigation, compass reading, boat maintenance, and other useful things.

In the summer of 1940, our whole troop and two leaders made a trip on a longboat. We traveled upriver, with our bicycles and gear on board. Sometimes when the boat anchored, we bicycled through small villages and explored the countryside, wearing our Girl Scout uniforms.

Our Girl Scout clubhouse, Het jonge schaap *("The Young Sheep"), 1940. (Photograph by Miep de Wit)*

One day, when we were happily bicycling on a narrow road on top of a dike, a car full of German soldiers and officers stopped us. One of the officers started to yell and scream at one of our leaders. I heard him tell her that all of us would be arrested because we were Scouts. Scouting was an organization from England, the

Our Girl Scout troop waiting to board the longboat, 1940. I am standing, fifth from the left. (Photograph by Miep de Wit)

Sitting in a meadow, looking at wildflowers and practicing knots, 1940. (Photograph by Miep de Wit)

Some of us from the Girl Scout troop looking at wildflowers, 1940. I am to the right. (Photograph by Miep de Wit)

enemy. Carla, a friend of mine, and I looked at each other, quite scared. We looked at Miep, one of our leaders, and saw her face turn white. We looked at our other leader, Ann, whose face was beet red. I held on to my bike's handlebars very tightly and watched the German officer.

"Kommen sie mitt!" ("Come along!") I heard him shout to our leader. Miep stayed where she was, calmly explaining in excellent German that she would not leave us, that she was responsible

for us, that we were young and innocent little girls, doing no harm at all, just having a nice holiday.

The German officer then ordered her to give him our names and addresses. The leaders' bikes were confiscated, but we were allowed to keep ours. We went back to the boat and then had to travel home immediately.

—♦—

Holland is a small country, and news traveled fast. In no time at all our parents found out what had happened.

After the encounter with the Germans we continued to get together. We never wore our Girl Scout uniforms, though, and when we met it was in each other's homes. Our wonderful windmill, the Young Sheep, stood empty.

9

HOARDING

When food supplies diminished, we had to use coupons to buy our groceries. I would go to the store and buy sugar, flour, coffee, and other staples, but often I was not able to get everything on my list.

Our meals became simpler every day. We grew accustomed to not having dessert. We soon were not able to buy meat, fish, or tea. The better foods were confiscated by the German occupants.

One food item I loved to buy for my family, when it still was available, was dark syrup, widely used as a replacement for sugar. I was sent with a white stoneware pitcher to the dim little grocery store. Full of anticipation, I entered the store, which smelled of licorice, tobacco, and apples.

"Good morning," I said. "Can I get a pound of syrup?"

"Good morning," the gray-haired old man answered from behind the low, worn oak counter. He walked to a huge barrel filled with syrup in the corner of his store, holding my white pitcher in one hand. With his other hand he dipped a ladle into the barrel. He took the ladle out and without even wasting one drop, poured the dark syrup into the stoneware pitcher, filling it exactly to the top. He then quickly swirled the ladle around and put it back into the barrel. He weighed the filled pitcher on his brass scale: "One and one-half pounds," he said. "One pound syrup and one-half pound for the pitcher." I was very impressed and looked around some more.

On the counter was a funny-looking metal box with a small hole in the top. I stuck my right index finger into the hole. It hurt a lot and when I quickly pulled my finger out, it was bleeding badly so I stuck my finger into my mouth. I did not know that men put their freshly purchased cigars into that box to snip off the tips so they could smoke the cigars right away.

My mother had given me one penny for myself, and after a long time I made the big decision to buy a penny's worth of salt licorice. The gray-haired store owner said, "Hold out your hand." I held out my left hand, and he filled it with one penny's worth of salt licorice.

"Left-handed?" he said. I mumbled something, thanked him, and quickly left the store, finger in my mouth, holding the pitcher and my half-melted licorice in my left hand. I walked home very carefully so as not to spill a drop of syrup.

Food and everything else eventually became so short of supply that most people started hoarding.

I remember an old lady who wanted to hoard something. There wasn't any more food to buy,

The fishermen in the small fishing village of Volendam hoarded fish and other treasures in their baggy pants and smuggled the goods wherever needed. (Courtesy of the author)

and the only thing left on the shelves was black shoe polish in small tin boxes. She bought 324 tins of the shoe polish and was very happy with her large purchase.

My parents bought Dutch chocolate bars and hid them in secret places. When a birthday, a holiday, or an important occasion arose, we had a candy bar for a treat. But the supply ran out, and eventually there were no longer any chocolate bars hidden away.

10

FAMILY ANTIQUES

JUNE 1941. ALL JEWS WERE LAID OFF FROM PUBLIC OFFICES. RACIAL DISCRIMINATION STARTED TO BECOME OBVIOUS. REFERENCES TO THE DUTCH ROYAL FAMILY WERE PROHIBITED. THE GERMANS BEGAN TO DRAFT YOUNG DUTCHMEN INTO THE GERMAN ARMY AND TO CONFISCATE ANYTHING THAT COULD BE USED IN THE WAR EFFORT.

In October 1941, the Germans ordered the Dutch people to deliver all their antique copper, brass, and pewter bowls, vases, serving pitchers, plates, and other metal treasures to a central gathering place. All those possessions were to be melted down to make ammunition. Some Dutch people complied, but much digging was done in gardens behind houses to bury precious family heirlooms.

My father had a different idea. He and I went out on an early evening, with sacks full of vases, kettles, and plates, to the church, which, fortunately, was only a few steps from our house. We sneaked in through a side door and started to climb the stairs.

It was easy at first, in spite of our heavy sacks. As we climbed higher, the stairs narrowed. It became darker and difficult to see.

We had almost reached the tower when the church bell rang. The deep tone of the heavy church bell vibrated through the attics as we climbed higher on the creaky ladders. We heard strange noises, the rush of things flying by—the place was full of bats—and we heard the hoot of a night owl.

Close to the top we found great hiding places between the floor joists, and we stuffed our antiques there.

The church bell rang again, now so close to our heads that the sound nearly deafened us and the vibrations were so strong that we had to hold on to the violently shaking ladders.

After the ringing stopped we climbed just a few rungs higher and reached the bell tower, where we peeked through the louvers and saw our town down below. In the far distance we heard the sound of machine guns and the explosion of a bomb dropped from a plane.

But how peaceful it was in the twilight, high up in the

tower. How quiet and restful and how uneventful life seemed seen from above. More night owls flew by; the sun was setting. I would have liked to have stayed up there for a long time.

The church in Zaandam where my father and I hid our antiques, illustrated here in about 1930. (Courtesy of Kerkvoogdy, Hervormde Gemeente Zaandam)

WHERE DID IT GO?

The kettles, plates, the golden rings,
The silver spoons and other things,
The copper, pewter, pots from brass,
Including even Grandma's vase,
All had to be brought to a certain place,
To a German with a happy face.

None of the treasures now would last,
'Cause melting down is going fast.
Cheap bullets could quick be produced
From all the heirlooms the Dutch had used.

But in the garden in the back
A hole was dug and in a sack,
All copper, pewter, silver, gold,
As much the sack and hole could hold
Was buried in the dark at night.

Not many bullets made to fight
The Germans got and they were mad.
The Dutch, however, were not sad.
They still had all their treasures near
And laughed about it without fear.

A Dutch poem, translated by author,
and a cartoon from a booklet, 1942.
(Courtesy of the author)

11

Threatening Happenings, 1942

In 1942, the Germans, anticipating attacks from the North Sea, started to fortify the coast. Students and older men from the occupied countries were recruited for forced labor. Those who resisted became prisoners of the Germans, and many were shot.

When I was sixteen, we moved to Dordrecht, a town that was one-half hour by train from Rotterdam. World War II had been raging for two years. Many times sirens wailed to warn everyone to take shelter. Often Allied planes flew overhead and sometimes they dropped bombs to attack German strongholds.

On one of those days, when the sirens gave their warning, students and teachers in my school went down to the basement to take shelter, but I sneaked upstairs so I could watch the Allied planes. I saw bombs fall, one after the other. The bombs looked like small specks, and when they reached the ground a huge cloud of smoke exploded into the sky. Then I heard a loud rumble, but I was too far away to see flames. More planes came, and more and more bombs fell on Rotterdam. At night the bombing stopped.

The next morning most of the survivors left the ruins of what had been a great city. They tried to find a place to live. Some families traveled to Dordrecht. The children from Rotterdam were enrolled in our schools, and a new girl by the name of Ine came to my class. Ine did not talk at all and after some time she put her arms on her desk and buried her head in her arms. It was very quiet in the classroom. We heard her whisper, "It all burned, and there was no water to stop the burning."

12

CURFEW

After we had been occupied for two years, the Germans established a curfew in order to eliminate the pursuing of illegal activities after sundown. It became an exciting game for me and my friends to sneak out in the dark. We hid in shadowy places, used back alleys, and were constantly on the alert for unfamiliar sounds. When we heard heavy footsteps, we knew that they probably were the footsteps of German soldiers, and it would be wise to hide quickly.

My mother was unaware of those evening adventures, as she was bedridden and did not leave her bedroom at all. My father sometimes noticed our escapades, but he himself occasionally stole out of the house to deliver something or maybe just to get some fresh air, as he always took care of my mother.

My sister was a librarian and kept her regular day hours, then came home and read or straightened the house. By now we did not have a maid or a gardener anymore; it was too expensive. All extra money had to be used to buy things to eat, often at incredibly high prices.

One Friday, at six P.M., one hour before curfew time, I left our home, the seventeenth-century parsonage overlooking the harbor, after a supper of one potato, some cabbage, and a little bit of gravy left over from Sunday.

The tide was high, and the water nearly reached the street in front of our house. The wind was strong, and the seagulls were lamenting, diving, and landing on the pilings. They glanced at me, then ignored me.

I thought about how lovely it would be to be a seagull, free from the heavy burden of a sick mother I could not talk to, and free from the war, which was always there, like a black shadow.

My classmates and I, all seniors, were going to meet at our favorite teacher's home. We were studying Shakespeare's *Hamlet*—secretly—as the Germans did not allow the study of the English language.

The small country of Holland is surrounded by several other countries where different languages are spoken. For this reason everyone in Holland was taught early on in school French, German, and English, in addition to the language spoken in Holland, which is Dutch.

We never traveled together to our secret meeting. It was too dangerous for several people to enter a home at the same time because the gathering could be construed by the Germans as an illegal meeting. So one by one each of us went to the side door,

Houder dezes
is heden per spoor te Dordrecht aangekomen.
Tengevolge van treinvertraging kan hij (zij) zijne (haare) woning
niet voor 24 uur bereiken.

N.S.12 01 02

De Hoofdstationschef   27.JUN.1943

DORDRECHT P.G.

Curfew excuse. If trains were delayed and we could not be at home before curfew, a statement was issued by the train station manager, which could be shown to the Germans if we were stopped by them. (Courtesy of author)

knocked four times quickly, stopped shortly, and then knocked twice more.

Mr. Visser, tall and lanky, cracked the door and let us in, one at a time. We sat on the cold floor in his living room. Mr. Visser had, as most of us, no more coal to fill and burn his coal stove with. We all had dressed as warmly as we could, with thick wool socks, wool sweaters, and hats and coats, which we kept on inside the house.

The curtains were closed so that no light could be seen from the outside, even though there was just one small lamp burning inside. It was hard to read under this sparse light, but we had memorized our parts and we acted them out, often halting, as we did not understand all the words and sentences.

Mr. Visser explained everything that puzzled us. He taught us so well, and we enjoyed his clarity and his knowledge of Shakespeare. Besides, he was so handsome with his deep, dark eyes and his curly black hair. We girls, of course, all had secret crushes on him.

At eight P.M. we took a short break from the *Hamlet* reading and talked about the happenings around us. We discussed the strange disappearance of a few of our classmates and the bombing of Rotterdam.

I had learned to speak about the war in a neutral sort of way, because I never knew if it was safe to express strong opinions, even to my classmates. Maybe someone in my group was in agreement with the German philosophy and could get the rest of us into trouble.

After our break we continued practicing our English and reading *Hamlet,* but suddenly we realized that it was now three hours past curfew time! Mr. Visser, who was always quoting from different plays, recited: "'All the world's a stage, and all the men and women merely players; they have their exits and their entrances . . .'"[4] and with a smile he added, "now you will exit our stage and enter a different world; be aware of danger and be safe."

I went out into the dark, chose narrow alleys to walk through, and listened for unusual sounds.

I was close to my home when I heard a faint cry in the darkness. Coming closer, I heard more cries and pleas. I heard shouting and harsh commands in German: *"Schnell einsteigen, wir gehen nach . . ."* ("Get in quickly, we are going . . .") I could not hear the last words, but I saw in the dark street close to my home, by the light of a flashlight held by a soldier, members of a Jewish family being pushed into a truck by Germans. The flashlight held by the soldier shone on the street for a short moment, and I had to duck so that the light would not shine on me. Then for a second the light paused on a girl's face. It was Rebecca, one of my classmates.

I swallowed hard. It seemed that something snapped inside me. I went home, very quietly entered my room in the old parsonage, and stared through the small window at the sky. My tears flowed silently for a very long time.

13

JOINING THE RESISTANCE, 1943

THOUSANDS OF JEWS WERE ARRESTED, CHAINED TOGETHER WITH
IRON CHAINS, PUT ON TRAINS TO TRANSPORT CAMPS IN VUGT AND
WESTERBORG, AND SENT FROM THERE TO CONCENTRATION CAMPS
IN GERMANY. MANY NON-JEWISH DUTCHMEN PROTESTED BY PAR-
TICIPATING IN HUGE PARADES. THEY MARCHED IN TIGHT COLUMNS
IN AMSTERDAM. THE GERMAN TANKS CIRCLED AROUND THEM,
BUT HESITATED TO SHOOT.

After high school I enrolled in the Academy for Physical Education in Amsterdam. My family had moved back from Dordrecht,
in the south of Holland, to Zaandam, very close to Amsterdam,
and I rented a room with a girlfriend from the academy. I had
trouble concentrating on studies because there was so much
happening all around us.

Life for the Jewish population became constantly more
dangerous. The Jews were ordered to wear yellow six-pointed stars
on their clothing. They were ordered to live in ghettos—huge,
enclosed areas in large cities. They were not allowed to come and

Enrolled at the Academy for Physical Education in Amsterdam as a freshman in 1942. I am in the second row from the bottom, at the far left. (Courtesy of the author)

go. Then a few Jews at a time were taken from their homes and later, together with many hundreds of others, they were put on trains and transported to Germany. Thus thousands upon thousands ended up in concentration camps.

We heard whispers of concentration camp sufferings. Stories filtered through, and some Jewish students at the academy strangely disappeared. Doris, a Jewish student, told me how some of her family members had been picked up by Germans and how she feared for their lives. She whispered that there were chambers in concentration camps in Germany where people were gassed to death. She told me about the skin of dead people being used to

Enrollment card for the Academy for Physical Education in Amsterdam. (Courtesy of the author)

make lamp shades. She told me that she could not see me anymore, as she had to go into hiding.

—♦—

One night when I came home from Amsterdam during a break from my schooling, I once again overheard a conversation in my father's study, this one between him and an older woman. They were whispering, and I picked up the word "underground." Then I knew that my father was the kind of man who would be involved in the Resistance, and it made me feel very good. When the meeting ended and the woman left, I secretly followed her in the dark to her house. Maybe this was my chance to work against the enemy.

She lived across a bridge, on the other side of town, in a simple room behind a small vegetable store. I knocked on her door. When she opened it just a crack, I introduced myself, and she let me in.

The small vegetable store in Zaandam, 1986. The woman who introduced me to the Resistance group lived here in 1940. (Courtesy of the author)

I told her I wanted to join the underground forces. She looked at me and said, "I want you to go back to your studies and think about it for a long time. There is nothing adventurous or romantic about working against the enemy—it is incredibly hard work. Your life would not be yours anymore. Go back to your studies and maybe forget about it. You are very young." I left disappointed, her words resonating in my mind, and returned to Amsterdam and my studies.

—⬦—

The situation became more grave as the war continued. We students in Amsterdam heard stories about incidents involving not only Jewish people, but also about students being taken to Germany against their will, and about the executions of political leaders in Holland.

About three months after my first conversation with the older woman in the vegetable store, I went back to her and told her that there was no doubt in my mind, I still wanted to join the underground.

"Very well," she said. "Tomorrow you will meet Piet in the square in front of the Protestant Church at exactly nine A.M. He will wear a brown wool hat and a gray raincoat. He will have a newspaper under his right arm and a shopping basket in his left hand. You will introduce yourself as Ellie. Good luck and be careful. Do not ever talk about what you are doing, including to your own family."

After hearing those simple words, I left her. I did not sleep very well that night. I was repeating softly the things the old woman had told me: Nine A.M. in front of the Protestant Church, gray raincoat, brown hat, newspaper, shopping basket, Piet. Nine A.M. shopping basket, brown hat, Protestant Church, nine A.M. . . . Finally I fell asleep, but woke up early and paced the floor until it was time to go. I carried my books and my tennis racket with me, so my family would think I was going back to school.

Full of anticipation and a little bit nervous, I headed for the square and spotted Piet immediately. He was indeed in the right place at the right time, wearing a gray raincoat, a brown hat, holding a newspaper under his right arm and a shopping basket in his left hand. He gave me my first assignment: I was to bring some identification papers and food coupons to a Jewish family hidden in an old house in the town of Haarlem. He also handed me a falsified I.D.: My new name was Ellie Van Dyk.

On that day my life changed completely. I rarely attended classes anymore. At night I was told where to meet my contact the next morning to receive new instructions, and which code words to use when approaching him or her. I was given a different assignment each day transporting Jewish people from one place to another, safer spot. Often we had to separate the children from their parents. I traveled with the children on trains and boats to the countryside, to the safer hiding places on farms, where the Germans rarely went. Quite a few of those children—unaware of their families' fate—stayed in the countryside until the end of the war in 1945. Many farmers' families "adopted" the Jewish children and treated them as their own. They went to school with the other children in the villages.

One problem was that clothing was getting scarce and the winter always seemed to get colder. Jewish people going into hiding ("underwater," as we called it) had to take the star off their coats. But cloth fades, and most old overcoats—which were so necessary during the cold winters—showed an obvious unfaded star-shaped spot. We always feared that star-shaped spot would be a dead giveaway and just hoped that it would not be noticed. Some women ingeniously took material from the inside hem of the old coats and sewed pockets over the faded spot. Others wore wool scarves over their coats, while still others held a newspaper to hide the spot. Then there were people who did not take any of these precautions and didn't get caught. Several times, however, while walking or traveling with us, Jews were arrested by some observant German. If that happened, we had to pretend we did not know the arrested person. Other Resistance workers told me about tragic incidents, but fortunately none of my Jewish traveling companions were ever caught.

14

TRAVELING TO
THE COUNTRYSIDE, 1943

ALL PERFORMING ARTISTS WERE REQUIRED TO BELONG TO A
GERMAN UNION. JEWISH ARTISTS WERE BANNED AND NOT
ALLOWED TO PERFORM ANYMORE. A NEW ORDER CAME FROM THE
GERMANS: DANCING WAS FORBIDDEN, TRUMPET PLAYERS WERE
NOT ALLOWED TO SWAY THEIR BODIES, ONLY MUTED TRUMPETS
COULD BE USED, AND HIGH NOTES COULD NOT BE PLAYED, AS THE
SWAYING OF BODIES AND THE HIGH SOUNDS RESEMBLED "NEGRO
MUSIC."

It was early in the morning and I dressed quickly and warmly. At
seven A.M. I had to meet a Jewish couple, musicians who had
played in the symphony in Amsterdam. I was to transport them to
a village in the province of Friesland, where they were to be met
and taken to a safe place on a farm.

When I arrived at the given address, I knocked three
times hard and twice softly (a code knock) on the door. A smiling
Dutch woman opened the door and let me in. "I will miss them,"
she said. "They have been good company for my husband and me,

but there are too many German soldiers around lately walking the streets. It is better for our guests to move on." As she spoke I followed her up two flights of stairs, through a linen closet, which had a small door inside, and into a room, where the curtains in front of the windows were closed. A Jewish man and woman, both pale and nervous, were waiting.

"Hello," I said, "Are you ready to go?" They embraced their Dutch hostess and followed me through the linen closet, down the stairs, and out into the street. Each was carrying a small shopping basket in which they had packed all their belongings.

I walked ahead, pretending not to know them, and they followed. The wind was blowing hard, and the man's hat blew off. He had lots of grayish-black, curly, rather long hair, and the wind blew his hair high around his head. He ran after his hat, grabbed it, and put it firmly on his head, holding it with one hand so he wouldn't lose it again.

We rode a trolley car to the Central Station, where I went to a ticket window and bought three round-trip tickets (the couple would only travel one way, but in case of a question they could say they were visiting a friend). I quickly handed their tickets to them, and we went to a platform where a train was waiting to take us to the northern part of the province of North Holland.

When we boarded the train we saw several compartments occupied by German officers. We walked through the corridors and finally found a compartment with only two older women sitting in it. The Jewish couple, immediately after sitting down, closed their eyes and pretended they were asleep. Suddenly a German officer opened the door of the compartment and hollered, "I.D. *bitte*." ("I.D. please.") All of us pulled out our I.D. cards, he looked at them and looked at us, and compared photos with faces, and looked again. Though shaky inside, I pretended to be calm. The Jewish couple, however, seemed visibly shaken. How could the officer not detect our fear?

After what seemed an eternity, the German handed our I.D. cards back to us and said with a smile, *"Danke schön und gute Reise."* ("Thank you very much and have a good trip.") Neither he nor the two older women in our compartment had noticed anything amiss.

After about one hour the train stopped in the middle of some meadows. Passengers leaned out of the windows to see why the train had stopped. German soldiers were hollering and shouting commands. We heard that a small bridge had

I.D. card. (Courtesy of the author)

been slightly damaged, and the train could not safely cross it. We had to get out of the train and carefully walk, one after the other, over the damaged bridge. All three of us dreaded the watchful eyes of the German soldiers, but miraculously we crossed the bridge and boarded a waiting train on the other side without any problems.

We finally reached Enkhuizen, an ancient harbor town, where the brisk wind from the sea was blowing so hard that we had to hold on to hats, skirts, and scarves. We walked with farmers and their families to the ferry boat. The farmers were holding baskets full of chickens, purchased at the open-air market.

Many fishermen who made the trip across the inland sea to sell fish at the Enkhuizen market walked toward the boat, their baskets now filled with fresh produce to bring home.

We boarded the ferry boat and settled down rather close to each other, but not together. We ate some pieces of bread, bought some imitation coffee, then closed our eyes. The wind was blowing hard, and the ferry boat bounced on the waves. The Jewish woman began to look gray-green, but never spoke. The passage on the inland sea was uneventful, and after two hours we reached the northeast coast of Holland.

We stepped ashore, again under the watchful eyes of German officers, and went to a small waiting room. I wore a bright blue scarf and red mittens and was approached by a young man who wore a red scarf and blue wool gloves. The young man said, "Did you have a good trip? I am so happy to see you again. Come on, and we will have some coffee."

I told him, "The trip was good, and I brought my aunt and uncle with me, so they can see a little bit of the countryside."

"Great!" he said. "You are very welcome."

After our coffee, the four of us left the small waiting room and climbed on a farm cart pulled by a horse. After about fifteen minutes of silent travel, the young man looked around. Nobody was in sight, and he stopped. He let me off the cart and then continued on with the Jewish couple.

I returned to the ferry boat on foot and started my long journey back to Amsterdam, very relieved that all had gone well that day.

15

THE STORY OF MARTIN

One of my many assignments was to bring a small boy, Martin, to the countryside. His parents had to stay in another place, and it was a heartbreaking farewell. I practically had to tear them apart and I could not cry, even though I wanted to. One always had to appear cool, brave, and confident.

We found little Martin a safe place in the country and had to cut off contact between him and his parents immediately. I often wondered what happened to Martin and his father and mother.

In June 1945, after the war had ended, my family was reading a newspaper called *Free Netherlands* printed in England for the Dutch people abroad. In it was an article about the normal daily happenings in Holland during the war—a sample of underground life. When my parents read the article about a little boy and his family, they realized it was also about me.

EEN GOEDE vriend en collega in het vaderland vertelde: "Dezer dagen liep ik professor Zoo-en-zoo tegen het lijf. Hij is, zooals je weet, een groot historicus. Hij heeft kans gezien er het leven van af te brengen ofschoon de Duitschers hem geducht op de hielen hebben gezeten;—en terecht, van *hun* kant gezien dan altijd. Nu is hij opgedoken en was blij, dat hij me zag. 'Beste vriend,' zei hij tegen me, 'jij hebt als journalist een belangrijke taak te vervullen, jij en alle andere menschen, die langs den weg zwerven en de kunst van observeeren verstaan. Schrijf alles op, waaruit zou kunnen blijken hoe het volk op de bezetting heeft gereageerd. Uitdrukkingen, moppen, bittere en goedmoedige spot. Liedjes, al zijn ze nog zoo kreupel en nog zoo krom. Leg dat vast en geef het in handen van de vakhistorici. Toekomstige geschiedkundigen zullen je dankbaar zijn voor dit nu nog zoo eenvoudig werk. Want wat weten wij historici bijvoorbeeld van de wijze, waarop het gewone volk der Nederlanden heeft gereageerd op den Franschen tijd en op de gebeurtenissen in de jaren, die op de landing bij Scheveningen volgden? Niets, hoegenaamd niets. Nu is het nog tijd dit gebrek te voorkomen, wanneer eenmaal de geschiedenis van onzen tijd zal worden bestudeerd.'"

De collega, die mij dit gesprek vertelde, voegde er aan toe, dat hij de wenk ter harte had genomen. En niet alleen hij, maar ook anderen. Zij stonden versaasd over de rijkdom van den oogst.

*

Aangemoedigd door dit gesprek, wil ik in de Kantteekeningen deze week een doodgewone geschiedenis vertellen. Zij speelt in mijn naaste omgeving. Zij kan den landgenooten te Londen een kijkje geven op het leven in Nederland tijdens de bezetting. De ruwe omtrekken van dat leven *kennen* we, de bijzonderheden kennen we *niet*.

Nauwelijks in Amsterdam gearriveerd, werd ik aangeklampt door een familielid. De vrouw vroeg mij of ik haar behulpzaam kon zijn bij het zoeken naar haar zoontje. Toen de Duitschers hun maatregelen tegen Joodsche Nederlanders waren begonnen, was het hele gezin ondergedoken. De vrouw had het kind drie jaar geleden afgegeven bij vrienden. Zij en haar man waren in drie jaar tijds 20 keer van adres veranderd. Met naam en foto hadden zij in het politieblad gestaan. Er werd voortdurend naar hen gezocht. Eén maal waren ze gearresteerd en in een politiebureau opgesloten, maar een brave politieman hielp hen ontsnappen door een W.C. raam. Zeventien maanden lang hadden zij elken nacht geslapen in een geheime slaapplaats, tusschen den vloer en de zoldering van de kamer daaronder, in het huis van een hunner vrienden. De man was drie jaar niet uit de kamer geweest. Al dien tijd hadden zij slechts nu en dan eene mondelinge boodschap gekregen dat het met hun zoontje goed ging. Veel geruststelling hadden die mededeelingen echter niet verschaft. Ze kenden den schuilnaam van een meisje, dat werkte in de kinderorganisatie die zich belast had met het transport van Joodsche kinderen en er waren geruchten

tot hen doorgedrongen, dat deze moedige jonge vrouw door de Gestapo was gepakt. Wel is waar werd er aan toegevoegd dat ze geen woord had losgelaten, ondanks alle martelingen die men haar had doen ondergaan, maar eenige zekerheid was niet te verkrijgen.

Nu was dan eindelijk Nederland bevrijd. De beide ouders konden zich vrij bewegen. De speurtocht naar hun jongetje dat drie jaar geleden was verdwenen, begon.

De jonge vrouw uit de geheime organisatie waarvan ze nooit meer hadden geweten dan dat ze "Ellie" heette, was spoedig genoeg gevonden. Ze bleek de dochter te zijn van een dominee. Ze had inderdaad in de organisatie gewerkt. Ze reisde namelijk op een bepaald spoorwegtraject heen en weer en gaf de kinderen volgens een soort estafettesysteem van de eene schakel naar de andere door. Haar informaties hielpen dus niet veel. Omdat een oorlogscorrespondent zich nu eenmaal gemakkelijker kan bewegen dan een gewoon burger, hadden ze nu mijn hulp ingeroepen.

We reden langs vele adressen en kwamen eindelijk te land bij een braven kantoorbediende, die tijdens de bezetting als ontvangststation had gediend voor kinderen, die moesten verdwijnen. Hij herinnerde zich het geval inderdaad, toen enkele bijzonderheden konden worden opgegeven die hij kon nakijken op een groezelig papiertje, dat drie jaar lang op een onmogelijke plaats verborgen had gelegen. Het resultaat in het bevolkingsregister officieel staat ingeschreven als Martin, droeg de naam Jopie toen hij op een ontvangststation werd afgeleverd.

Dat was in elk geval het begin van de draad die ons door een langen dichthof tenslotte naar het kind zou kunnen leiden. Ik sla nu maar een paar schakels over om te vertellen dat we tenslotte belandden bij een braven metaalbewerker, die ons een adres gaf te Sneek. De kinderen uit de groep waartoe Jopie behoord, waren allemaal in Friesland ondergebracht en het knooppunt in die provincie was een handelsreiziger aldaar.

Den volgenden dag zijn we naar Sneek getogen. De handelsreiziger woonde in een klein huisje. Een belangrijk gedeelte van de huiskamer werd in beslag genomen door een orgel; op het orgel stond een bundel stichtelijke gezangen. Het gezin is een eenvoudig, oerdegelijk Friesch gezin.

O ja, de handelsreiziger herinnerde zich het geval wel. De naam Jopie zeide hij beslist, maar men moest niet van hem verlangen dat hij wist waar het kind was opgeborgen. In de eerste plaats was dergelijke wetenschap veel te gevaarlijk. In de tweede plaats had hij in den loop der jaren meer dan 200 kinderen door zijn handen laten gaan. Al die kinderen werden een paar dagen in dat huisje te Sneek gelogeerd. Dan werden zij door de organisatie ergens op het Friesche platteland ondergebracht. Het laatste halfjaar had de handelsreiziger en zijn gezin zelf moeten onderduiken.

Een dijkwachter die ergens in het Noorden dienst deed, bleek de man te

zijn die den sleutel tot tal van deze raadselkinderen in handen had. In Friesland werkt de telefoon gelukkig nog. Hij werd van zijn werk gebeld, zei dat hij direct op de fiets naar huis zou gaan en met een half uurtje weer op zou bellen. Hij hield zich prompt aan deze afspraak. Jopie zat verborgen te Westergeest, vlakbij Kollum, als ik het wel heb, 8 k.m. van de Lauwerszee.

*

De pleegmoeder van Jopie bleek een doodarme weduwe te zijn. Ze woonde in een klein huisje vlakbij de vaart. Toen de moeder van Jopie het huis binnenkwam zat het kind juist te eten. Hij keek op, werd lijkbleek en riep: "Mèm"!

Jopie, het ondergedoken Joodsche jongetje uit Amsterdam, sprak Friesch of hij van zijn leven nooit anders had gesproken.

De pleegmoeder lachte en huilde tegelijk. Jopie had haar al die jaren de eenzaamheid doen vergeten. Jopie was haar oogappel geworden, een fiksche boerenknaap van elf jaar die te wijdbeensch op zijn klompen stond. Elke ochtend om 7 uur was hij in den winter er op uit gegaan om houtjes te sprokkelen voor Tante . . . Hij zong in het kerkkoor en hij vocht met de jongens en kende op zijn kinderlijke manier alles van het boerenbedrijf.

Het werd een ontroerend halfuurtje. Jopie's spullen werden ingepakt, een paar oude broekjes, een paar versleten schoenen, een bijbeltje en een gezangboek. Jopie beloofde veel te zullen schrijven aan Tante en Tante liet haar tranen den vrijen loop. De geheime organisatie had Tante elke week 12½ gulden uitgekeerd voor het onderhoud van het kind, maar de toekomstige inkomstenderving kon haar niets schelen, want Jopie was haar alles. Of Jopie zijn moeder, vroeg ze, eens wilde uitkijken in Amsterdam waar misschien ook kwam ze wel naar de hoofdstad wonen om een beetje dichter bij het kind te zijn.

Het zijn allemaal eenvoudige menschen, die dit werk van menschenliefde en heldenmoed hebben verricht. Hun namen hebben nooit in de krant gestaan. Ze zijn slechts doodgewone menschen met een orgeltje in huis en een bundeltje stichtelijke gezangen en aan de wand der Christelijke kalender. Maar zij zijn het staal van de natie, onverslijtbaar, onverwoestbaar, hard en onbuigzaam. Ze denken niet aan vernieuwing en aan verjonging, want precies als hun voorouders in den Tachtigjarigen Oorlog zijn zij zich aan de groote Waarheid, die vele honderden jaren geleden werd geopenbaard, bij duizenden.

Laten wij nederig getuigen, dat wij er trotsch op zijn het te mogen behooren tot hetzelfde volk als zij.

*

Zulke verhalen kan men in Nederland bij honderden hooren. Ik heb er dit nu maar uitgekozen omdat ik tot de ontknooping ervan persoonlijk heb kunnen bijdragen.

De historicus, waarvan ik in het begin van deze aanteekeningen gewaagde, had gelijk, toen hij mij als collega en vriend vroeg vast te leggen wat de gewone man tijdens de bezetting heeft gedaan. Deze

(Vervolg op bladz 622)

The newspaper article about Jopie and "Ellie," from **Vrÿ Nederland** *("Free Netherlands"), June 16, 194* *(Courtesy of the author)*

Here is the translation of the article:

I had just arrived in Amsterdam when I was approached by a family member. The woman asked me if I could help her to find her little boy. Three years earlier, when the Germans started to persecute the Dutch Jews, her whole family had gone into hiding. She brought her boy to friends. In those three years she and her husband had changed addresses 20 times. Their names and phone numbers had appeared in a police newspaper. Constant searching for them went on. Once they were arrested and locked up in a police station. With the help of a courageous policeman, they were able to escape through a small bathroom window. For 17 months of the 3 years they spent every night in a secret bedroom between floor and ceiling of the room underneath, in the house of some friends. During those years they had received only a few verbal messages that their little boy was fine, but that did not really ease their worries. They knew the name of a girl working in the children's organization who had the job of hiding Jewish children, and they had heard rumors that this brave young woman was picked up and put into prison by the Gestapo. Indeed—it was added—she had not mentioned anything to the Germans in spite of the tortures she was subjected to, but nothing definite was heard.

Now finally, the war was over and Holland was free. The boy's parents could move around again. They began the search for their child who had disappeared three years ago. Ellie, the young woman from the secret organization, was found rather soon. She was the daughter of a minister and had indeed worked in that organization. She had traveled on the railroad between certain towns and delivered children as in a relay system from one contact to another. She remembered an address in the province of Friesland. The parents and I stopped at this address first and met a brave office worker who had worked during the occupation in a receiving station for children who had to be hidden. He did indeed remember this particular case. When we gave him some details, he checked a small worn and dirty piece of paper, stuffed away for three years in a crack in bricks of his chimney. It stated that the boy, Martin, was now in the official population register under the name of Jopie. This was the first clue which finally led us through many wanderings to the child. After numerous tips, we arrived at a metalworker's house, and the owner gave us an address in Sneek. All the children of the group Jopie belonged to had found homes in the province of Friesland. The central key there was a traveling salesman. The next day we went to Sneek. The salesman lived in a very small house where the largest part of the living room was taken up by an organ. There were hymn books on top of the organ. The family was a very religious Frisian family. Oh yes, the salesman remembered this case. He knew the name Jopie, but he didn't remember where the boy had been taken. This knowledge would have been far too dangerous; if he were arrested, under the stress of interrogation, he may have revealed the information. Also, more than 200 Jewish children had gone through his home. The children had spent only a few days in his small house. Then members of the organization found different homes for them. During the last six months of the war, he himself had to go into hiding with his family because he was under suspicion of conducting illegal activities.

A dikewatcher, who worked in the north, was the man who had the key to the whereabouts of lots of these children. Fortunately, in Friesland, the telephones were still working. Phoned at work, he said he would bicycle home immediately and phone back within 30 minutes. He kept his word, phoned back and told us that Jopie was living in Westergeest, approximately eight miles away from the Northern Sea waters. We found Jopie living in a small house close to the canal with his adopted mother, a widow. When the boy's real mother walked inside, the child was eating porridge. He looked up, turned very white and shouted, "Mem!" ["Mother"].

The hidden little boy from Amsterdam spoke Frisian (a dialect of Friesland) as if he had never spoken anything else. His adopted mother laughed and cried at the same time. Jopie had, during all those years, helped her to forget her loneliness. He had become her pride and joy, a healthy farmboy of 11 years, who stood steady in his wooden shoes. Every morning, at 7 o'clock, he went out to chop firewood for "Auntie." He sang in the church choir, fought with the boys and knew in his childish way all about farming. It was a touching half hour!

Jopie's possessions were packed: a couple of pairs of worn-out pants, a pair of old shoes, a small Bible and a hymn book. Jopie promised to write to Auntie, and Auntie cried freely.

The secret organization had sent 12.50 guilders every week to Auntie for the upkeep of the child. Losing this income did not bother her at all, as Jopie was the apple of her eye. She asked Jopie's mother to look around in Amsterdam, to find a small house; perhaps she could move there to be a little closer to the child.

—*By a War Correspondent, June 1945, in* Free Netherlands

16

Treasures We Found

The pilots of the Allied planes often dropped newspapers on our country. They were flying over Holland on their way to the east, to Germany, where they were bombing German industries. It was a great way to keep us informed about what was happening in the war and in the world. The text was in English, which did not pose a problem for us, as we had studied English in school since we were young.

When we noticed papers scattered around, we considered ourselves very lucky. Sometimes we found the complete edition of the *London Weekly Times* printed in very small format.

We savored this news from England, but after reading the newspapers from beginning to end, we had to burn them rather than risk arrest. This copy, however, was saved by my family.

AIR MAIL EDITION

THE TIMES

WEEKLY EDITION

No. 3,545   Registered at the G.P.O. for transmission in the United Kingdom   LONDON WEDNESDAY DECEMBER 20 1944   The Postage for this Issue is: Inland 1½d; Abroad 1d   PRICE 4D

ALLIANCE

ASSURANCE   COMPANY LTD.

of Bartholomew Lane,   London, E.C.2

FIRE · LIFE · ACCIDENT ·   BURGLARY · MOTOR · MARINE · ETC.

The "Alliance" has representatives throughout the United Kingdom, the Dominions, the Colonies and elsewhere abroad.

HEAD OFFICE TEMPORARILY AT KIDBROOKE PARK, FOREST ROW, SUSSEX

NEWSPAPERS & MAGAZINES BY DAWSON'S

SPECIMEN ANNUAL RATES POST FREE

BRITISH   BRITISH (Cont.)   AMERICAN (Cont.)

AMERICAN

Send for a free Copy of our
"GUIDE TO THE PRESS OF THE WORLD"

W^{M.} DAWSON & SONS, L^{TD.}

ESTABLISHED 1809

Head Offices :—
43, WEYMOUTH STREET, LONDON, W.I, ENGLAND

Schweppes

TABLE WATERS
SQUASHES AND CORDIALS

Owing to wartime conditions these World-famed beverages are now in very short supply. We assure our Overseas friends that shipments will be resumed as soon as possible

Protectively Yours
JOHN TANN

THE OLDEST ESTABLISHED SAFE MAKERS IN THE WORLD
JOHN TANN LTD · LONDON · ENGLAND

Drambuie
PRINCE CHARLES EDWARD'S LIQUEUR

Shipments to overseas markets are suspended in the meantime owing to shortage of stocks. Exports will be resumed as soon as there is an improvement in the supply position.

The Drambuie Liqueur Co., Ltd.
12. York Place,
EDINBURGH.

Ailsa Craig
MARINE & INDUSTRIAL
DIESEL ENGINES

Half a century's experience is behind these fine ones and explains their world-wide reputation for perfect service in use. Write for details.

By Appointment to the late King George V.

AILSA CRAIG LTD,
Chiswick Works,
London, W.4.
Telephone:
Chiswick 0605.
Cables:
Ailscrater, London.

10-100 B.H.P. Diesel

BLANCO
WHITE CLEANER
IN BLOCKS, TUBES, BOTTLES
"Keeps white shoes white"

Sole Manufacturers :—
JOSEPH PICKERING & SONS, LTD.,
SHEFFIELD, ENGLAND. Estab. 1824

Exide
BATTERIES
for
CAR STARTING
and
LIGHTING

Efficiency with Long-life...

THE CHLORIDE ELECTRICAL STORAGE CO. LTD.
EXPORT DEPT.: GROSVENOR GARDENS HOUSE
GROSVENOR GARDENS, LONDON, S.W.I
Represented at : BOMBAY, CALCUTTA, JOHANNESBURG, S.A., WELLINGTON, N.Z. COPENHAGEN, DUBLIN, SINGAPORE AND SYDNEY

EX677B

PROSPERITY
AFTER VICTORY

PROSPERITY will depend on exports. Foreign markets which clamour for British engineering products for reconstruction must be held. Manufacturers who make full use of foreign-language catalogues, booklets, leaflets, etc., will be in a far better position to get a lasting grip on these markets. Williams, Lea & Co. specialise in this

work. They have large founts of display and text faces available, including Russian, Greek and Hebrew. Typesetting and proof-reading are carried out by nationals under British supervision. By entrusting your foreign-language printing to Williams, Lea & Co. you will keep the work in this country and secure absolute accuracy and correctness in every detail.

IF IT'S A PRINTING JOB

WILLIAMS, LEA
& COMPANY LIMITED

Colour and General Printers · Printers of Periodicals
Special Department for Foreign Languages

CLIFTON HOUSE, WORSHIP STREET, LONDON, E.C.2   Tel: Bishopsgate 8121-2-3-4

The December 20, 1944, edition of the London Weekly Times, printed in a very small format and dropped from Allied planes. The actual size of this newspaper is 5 3/8" x 8 1/4". (Courtesy of the author)

ADVANCING IN LEYTE

THE RE

A "duck" passing a crippled Japanese tank on a dusty road during the American advance into the interior of the island of Leyte. These amphibious vehicles have been invaluable during the Leyte campaign for crossing swamps and taking troops and stores to the front in terrain impassable to other vehicles.

Three pictures received by radio depicting incidents member of the parachute troops firing from the Act Marshal Alexander is shown leaving British headqu and, below on the right, parachute troop

IN HOLLAND AND BURMA : PROBLEMS FOR SAPPERS

Two phases of the work of the engineers in warfare. On the left men of the Indian Field Engineers of the 36th Division are seen searching with bare hands for mines and booby traps on the last stage of the advance to Pinwe in Burma. The other picture shows Royal Engineers filling in holes in a road in Holland with logs cut from a neighbouring wood.

FO

Thousands of letters and parcels hav show a busy scene in one of the Ar stockings, a favourite gift, at a spec

FOR SEA SUPPLY ROUTES

The top picture shows one of the new cargo ships specially designed for carrying military equipment. Below: Three of Britain's new "Tid" tugs, so called (short for "Tiddlers") because of their size

BRITISH LEADER IN ALBANIA

The story of the splendid work of the British troops who have been operating with partisans in Albania since April, 1943, has just been released. In this picture Brigadier G. M. O. Davy, who has been in command of the operations, is seen on a beach in Albania.

NEW ZEA

A brilliant success has been scored b Italy. They drove the 90th Panzer Gr town of Faenza on the road to Bologn the

THENS   # TRIBUTE TO U.S. ARMY

with the E.L.A.S. The largest picture shows a ...erating from the burning house seen below. Field-...ral Scobie during his brief visit to the Greek capital ... centres. Here they took 30 prisoners.

Lichfield has granted a depth of the U.S. Army the right of marching through the city on all ceremonial occasions "with drums beating, bands playing, Colours flying, and bayonets fixed." Outside the Guildhall, Lichfield, after the right had been recorded.

ST. VALERY AND THE HIGHLAND DIVISION
Pipes and drums of the 51st Highland Division taking part in a ceremony at St. Valery-en-Caux to mark three months of freedom from German occupation. It was a* St. Valery in 1940 that this division was forced to surrender after a valiant struggle. Men of the division retook the town four years later.

Mr. Philip Guedalla, the distinguished historical writer, who died in a London hospital on Saturday. He was 55.

A new postage stamp from New Zealand bearing a small surcharge for the Health Camps Fund. The design shows Princess Elizabeth and Princess Margaret in camp uniforms.

...rn front. Our pictures ...s critically examining ...Belgian Red Cross.

FOUR WINNERS OF THE VICTORIA CROSS
Captain J. N. Randle, The Royal Norfolk Regt., who has been awarded posthumously the V.C. for gallantry in Assam. Right: Three winners of the Victoria Cross after being decorated by the King at a recent Investiture. Left to right: Lieut.-Col. H. Foote (Royal Tank Regt.), Major R. Wakeford (The Hampshire Regt.), and L/Cpl. F. Jefferson (The Lancashire Fusiliers).

A GIFT TO HOLLAND
The Queen with Princess Juliana standing by one of the mobile canteens she has given for service in Holland. Altogether she handed over two "Queen's Messenger" convoys, 27 vehicles, to the Princess for the use of the Dutch Government. The ceremony took place at Buckingham Palace.

WRENS GO TO AUSTRALIA
Mr. S. M. Bruce, the High Commissioner for Australia in London, with members of the W.R.N.S. who are going to Australia. Three officers and 200 ratings form the first party.

h the Eighth Army in ...capture the important ...land troops are seen in

17

No Sounds While Hiding, 1944

I remember one Jewish family of eight who found shelter in a house in Haarlem. A hiding place was built for them under the floor. One day I was to deliver some food and other necessities to them and noticed before entering the house that one curtain was half open. I did not go in—it was a sign of trouble. Later, I was told that some Germans had temporarily moved into the house. This happened sometimes: If the soldiers noticed a place that seemed deserted, they made it their home for a long or short time.

The Jews under the floor could not make any noises—absolutely *none*. They were totally silent for a whole week, all eight of them. After the Germans left, seven came out of the hiding place, white and thin and very weak, but alive. One of them had died very quietly.

18

THE DOORBELL, 1944

Occasionally I came home from Amsterdam to see my family in Zaandam. The war went on and not many vendors made deliveries at my family's house anymore. Food was getting scarce and so was coal, and there was no more paper to print the daily news. But the flower vendor still came by every Friday morning, and if there was just a little bit of money left, people bought fresh flowers for the weekend.

The parsonage—my parents' home—was by no means empty. There always were people hiding there, usually Resistance workers, seeking refuge from the Germans. As did many homes in Holland, this home, too, had a wonderful hiding place. A trapdoor was cut out in our attic floor, and it opened into a rather roomy space, approximately seven by four feet, between the attic floor and the ceiling of the story underneath. The hiding place had some food and water and a small chamber pot. A person could not stand

upright in this secret hide-
away, but at least four people
could sit.

The doorbell still
rang often, in spite of the
short supply of food. There
were so many people suffering from sickness due to
hunger, so many who had
lost a family member because
of deportation or execution
by the Germans, so many
who were distraught because
a friend or relative had been
imprisoned. They all needed
spiritual help and encourag-
ing words from my father.

*The front of our home, the parsonage, in Zaandam. The
parsonage is the building in the middle of this picture taken
in 1986. (Photograph by Les Ippisch)*

But each time the doorbell rang, there was a panic
inside: All of the people who were hiding had to run quickly and
quietly up the first stairway—past the walls covered with lovely
delft blue tiles—up the second, creaky stairway to the attic. They
would quickly open the trapdoor and jump into the hiding place.
Then my sister would close the trapdoor, put a rug over it, and
walk calmly—though flushed—down the stairs to open the front
door.

In the beginning this happened once a week, perhaps,
and as the war went on, sometimes several times a day.

It became a contest for us to see how quickly this com-
motion could turn into total peace and quiet. This very serious
game against the clock helped to alleviate some of the tension. The
record was two minutes and twenty seconds—a feat we were all
incredibly proud of. Sometimes our guests were in the hiding place

for just a few minutes, other times longer. It depended on who rang the doorbell and how long the visitor talked to my father.

The Germans never became suspicious of the comings and goings at the parsonage. They took for granted that there were always people who wanted to speak to the minister.

19

THE SILENT DAY, SEPTEMBER 1944

The combined underground groups decided that it would be an enormous handicap for the Germans if the railroads did not operate anymore. Fuel was getting very scarce, and the Germans relied on train transportation to keep control over our occupied country.

Of course, it was equally hard for the Dutch to be without trains, but we knew we could exist without the railroads if we had to. We could ride our bikes.

The Dutch government in London arranged with the underground leaders to guarantee normal wages for all striking railroad workers. The wages would be distributed on a weekly basis by the NSF (National Relief Organization).

So, one day in September 1944, the railroad strike started. Not one man or woman went to work for the railroad system that morning—not one person. The whole country was totally silent, there were no sounds of trains anywhere, no hustle and bustle at railroad stations. All transportation was at a complete standstill except for biking or walking. The Germans had to rely totally on truck transport, which hampered their effectiveness very much, and they retaliated. They cut off supplies of food and fuel to all people in Holland.

Transporting Jewish people to new hideouts was now out of the question. They had to stay at their present hiding places and simply hope for the best. The trains never ran again until after the war was over.

20

A New Job

Occasionally I went back to the academy to attend some classes, as I was still officially enrolled. I also continued to rent a room in Amsterdam, but my heart wasn't in my studies. I wanted to continue to work for the Resistance.

By this time I knew quite a few people in the Resistance movement and I asked around for a new job. After about six weeks, while I was visiting my family in Zaandam, a gentleman named Mr. Buys approached me in front of our house and said, "If you want to work, come and follow me to Amsterdam tomorrow morning for a new job. Your name will be Miep."

The next day, at eight-thirty A.M., Mr. Buys led the way on his bicycle and I followed on mine. We pedaled over the dikes against the hard-blowing wind and arrived, after about an hour, in Amsterdam. The town was quiet; a few German trucks drove by. There were some people on bikes and others walking. I was wondering what my new job would be like.

We ended up on one of the streets along a canal, where

Walraven van Hall, leader of the Resistance forces in Holland, Banker of the Resistance, who became my new boss in September 1944. This photo was taken around 1939. During the war years he had many different names and changed his identity on a regular basis in order to elude the enemy. I knew him as "Uncle Piet" and as "Mr. van Tuyl." (Courtesy of the author)

the beautiful old homes with the typical Dutch gables are still standing. Dutch merchants had lived in these buildings in the seventeenth century.

I followed Mr. Buys down some steps to a basement room. A man was waiting for us, and I was introduced; he was called Mr. van Tuyl. He was thin and had a fascinating, strong face with piercing eyes, which sometimes, to my surprise, could be very gentle.

"Hello," he said. "You are going to be my new courier. One of your most important jobs is to find us a different meeting place in Amsterdam every Friday morning, when we meet at nine o'clock. Also, see if you can manage to get the place somehow heated a little bit and provide us with something to eat if possible. During the rest of the week you will do many errands for me, so you will have to be around most of the time. If you need money, tell me and I will get it for you. It would be good to wear different outfits often because the German SS [the German State Security Service] will perhaps follow you."

I was excited to be offered this new job, but also somewhat apprehensive. Could I do this new position justice? It entailed a great deal of responsibility, and I was young and inexperienced. It was the start of a new chapter in my life.

21

THE SECRET NETWORK

After four years of war, there were nine different Resistance organizations. There was a sabotage group, which was busy blowing
up bridges, killing Germans if necessary, freeing political prisoners if possible, destroying railroads, and stealing bicycles for us if
we needed them.

A complete underground printing organization called
The Busy Bee took care of falsifying papers, I.D.'s, food stamps,
publications, and so forth.

The National Relief Organization (NSF) handled all the
money. A good deal of money was needed to assist people in hiding, to give financial help to citizens who provided homes for
Jewish families, students in hiding, and Resistance workers, and
to quietly but effectively combat the occupational forces. The NSF
consisted mostly of very brilliant financiers and was, with the help
of secret radio transmissions, in daily contact with the Dutch government in exile in London.

There was also a group that assisted the Jews, found

289e Jaargang No 134

Bureaux: Groote Houtstraat 93.
Tel. Advert. 39701, Redactie 10699
Pungière 11088 Haarlemsche Ct. Haarlem
Bijkantoor, Soendaplein 37. Tel. 15830
Hoofdredacteur: F. C. Derks

Maandag 5 Juni 1944

Verschijnt dagelijks,
behalve op Zon- en Feestdagen
Drukkerij: Z. B. Spaarne 12. Tel. 10733
Kantoor IJmuiden: Kennemerlaan 88,
IJmuiden-Oost
Uitg.: Graf. Bedrijven, Damiate, Haarlem
K 1507

Haarlemsche Courant

Dit nummer verschijnt buiten verantwoordelijkheid van Mees, Peereboom en Derks.

Capituleert Duitschland ?

Artikel van Joseph Göbbels in Das vierte Reich.

„Capituleert Duitschland? Ziedaar een vraag, die velen bezig houdt." Aldus de Minister van Propaganda , in het binnenkort te verschijnen nummer van Das vierte Reich. „Ons antwoord op deze vraag is duidelijk", gaat Z. Exc. voort. — „Natuurlijk capituleert Duitschland. Wie daaraan twijfelt, is een dwaas. Dat wij den oorlog zullen verliezen, dat wij bezig zijn hem te verliezen en hem reeds verloren hebben, weet een kind. Ik ben er dan ook van overtuigd, dat ik niets nieuws aan het Duitsche publiek mededeel, wanneer ik het signaal van den Rijksregeering hier nog eens duidelijk neerschrijf. Duitschland verliest den oorlog. Ik heb daaraan echter nog iets toe te voegen en wel iets, dat de Engelsche en Amerikaansche plutocratenbende wel koud op hij zal vallen, wat de bolsjewistische horden zal doen verstarren van schrik, wat de tegenstanders van het Nationaal-Socialisme waar ter wereld ook voorgoed alle hoop zal ontnemen. Het is dit: **Wij verliezen dezen oorlog, omdat wij hem verliezen willen.** Laat niemand aan de waarheid dezer woorden twijfelen. Wat wij zeggen, is ons heilige ernst. Wij zijn niet gewend een gemuilbande pers leugenberichten te laten verkondigen, die we eenige weken weer gedementeerd moeten worden. Het is niet onze tactiek het Duitsche volk zand in de oogen te strooien. Wij hebben er nooit naar gestreefd den toestand gunstiger te teekenen, dan hij in werkelijkheid was. Het Duitsche volk heeft dit begrepen. Het kent ons. Het weet, wat het aan ons heeft. Inmiddels ontvluchten wij ons niet, zoo gaat de Minister voort, dat er, vooral in de bezette gebieden, nog lieden te vinden zullen zijn, wier gebrek aan kennis van onze Nationaal-Socialistische levensbeschouwing het onmogelijk maakt te begrijpen, waarom wij dezen oorlog willen verliezen. Voor hen, niet voor het politiek-rijpe Duitsche volk, is dus een nadere toelichting noodig. In de eerste plaats dan bedenke men, dat in het vijandelijke kamp al sinds Duinkerken de overtuiging leeft, dat deze oorlog door de zoogenaamde geallieerden niet meer gewonnen **kan** worden. Deze overtuiging is door de gebeurtenissen der laatste jaren tot zekerheid geworden. Wij zijn diep in Rusland binnengedrongen en zijn weer vrijwillig teruggegaan, nadat wij hadden laten zien, waartoe wij in staat zijn. Tot in de onmiddellijke nabijheid van Alexandrië trokken onze dappere mannen met onbuigzamen wil en ook daar zijn wij teruggekeerd na den vijand en zoo in het nauw te hebben gebracht, dat hij uit wanhoop tot het offensief van El Alamein overging. Op dezelfde wijze zijn wij uitgaande van hetzelfde vooraf opgemaakte plan, hebben wij Sicilië ontruimd. Spreken deze feiten niet voor zichzelf? Thans echter zijn

HEEL RUSLAND
gebruikt thans
PANKO
„ZE VLIEGEN ER UIT!!"

wij tot het hoogtepunt genaderd. De Anglo-Amerikaansche bandieten, wetend, dat hun strijd verloren is, werpen zich op de terreur. Duitsche steden worden vernietigd, Duitsche industrieën „in de prak" gegooid. Het zijn de laatste wanhoopsdaden van het uitgeputte Albion. Het zijn de doodsstuipen der Amerikaansche invasieridders. Weldra zal het uur gekomen zijn, dat hun voorraden zijn uitgeput, dat onze duikbooten de zee schoongeveegd hebben en elk schip, dat de vijandelijke vlag nog voert. Dan ligt Engeland op de knieën en smeekt om genade. Wat zou elke andere staat onder deze omstandigheden doen? Het antwoord op deze vraag is duidelijk. Niet echter voor den Führer, niet voor onze Duitsche Regeering. Zij beiden wijken af van den traditioneelen weg. Zij versmaden kapitalistische methoden. Zij slaan Engeland de laatste zekerheid uit de vuist. Engeland meent, dat het dezen oorlog zal verliezen.... welnu, de geschiedenis zal leeren, dat het zich ook nu weer vergist. Het zal den oorlog winnen! In strijd met al zijn verwachtingen, in strijd met zijn vaste overtuiging, zal Engeland dezen oorlog winnen, omdat net op dat moment Duitschland de wapens zal neerleggen.

Daar staat dan het perfide Albion met een zegepraal, waarop het geenszins heeft gerekend, waarmee het geen weg weet. Een panische angst zal het land en volk overvallen, angst voor de verantwoordelijkheid, angst voor de toekomst. Radeloos zullen de diplomaten trachten te redden wat er behoeft te redden valt, in aller ijl zullen de troepen oprukken... maar waarheen, tegen wien? Er zal geen vijand meer zijn. De slagen van het leger vallen in het luchtledige. Immers, de Duitsche troepen hebben reeds gecapituleerd, de vloot heeft zichzelf getorpedeerd als

Vervolg zie pag. 2

Hij wist met zichzelf geen raad.

En de maatschappij evenmin. Driemaal had hij gezeten wegens diefstal. Twee veroordeelingen had hij nog te wachten wegens mishandeling en roof. Zijn vrouw was van hem weggeloopen. Uit de ouderlijke macht was hij ontzet.

Wat zou het beste voor zijn toekomst zijn?

Wel, hij meldde zich als Landwachter. Nu was zijn toekomst verzekerd.

Duizenden schurken deden het, waarom gij niet?

TANKGRACHT
IN DE HAARLEMMERHOUT.
Ook voor dit cultuurmonument
strijden onze jongens aan het Oostfront.

AAN DE N.S.B.

Vervloekte bende, die „Heil Hitler!"
krijschend,
De straten onzer goede stad bevuilt,
Die altijd alles voor uzelve eischen
Van Volksverbondenheid en Socialisme
huilt;

Verraders, die de vrije Nederlanden
Hebt Duitschland in de grove muil
gespeeld,
Die thans met uwe bloedbevlekte handen
Nog dagelijks de besten onzer keelt;

Uw Nazidom zou onze vrijheid wezen !
Uw Nazidom zou onze toekomst zijn !
Eer stroomt geen water meer door onze
Rijn.
Eer maakt gij onze kinderen tot weezen,

Gij Godverlaten troep van Jodenbeulen
Gij lafaards zonder moed, fatsoen of eer,
Eer ooit mijn vaderland met u gaat heulen
Bestaat mijn land als Nederland niet meer.

Te wapen, Neêrland, tegen deze schelmen,
Want ieder hunner is een rasschavuit.
't Is niet genoeg, dat g'u niet laat
bedwelmen
Door hun gebazel ! Ga en roei ze uit !

G. PASUS.

BEKENDMAKING

D Höhere S.S.- und Polizeiführer maakt bekend:

Wederom zijn in Haarlem twee gevallen van sabotage voorgekomen, die des te ergerlijker zijn, dae de opnieuw de ophitsers buiten sch. zijn gebleven. Bovendien betref het hier gevallen van misdadigin van de Duitsche Weermacht, terwijl toch genoegzaam bekend mag worden verondersteld, dat daartegen met groote scherpte wordt opgetreden.

Op 15 Mei j.l. des middags omtrent twee uur heeft een hond van kenkelijk plutocratische huize zijn behoefte gedaan tegen de Mauermuur op den Wagenweg. Officieel is vastgesteld, dat ter dier plaats opzettelijk heeft uitgekozen In de onmiddellijke nabijheid immers zijn tal van boomen aanwezig en nu het prikkeldraad daaromheen is zoo gespannen, dat de hond, welks borsthoogte een schatting 75 cm bedroeg, er gemakkelijk onderdoor kon loopen. Een lid van de Duitsche Weermacht heeft bovendien persoonlijk geconstateerd, dat het dier te rechterachterpoot bij het verrichten van zijn laffe en beleedigende daad heeft opgelicht, terwijl het geacht kon worden te weten, dat in de Groot-Germaansche levensruimte bij het verrichten van viezigheid alléén de rechtervóórpoot mag worden opgeheven.

Betrouwbare getuigen, o. a. de heer Faber, die den door de genoemde Mauermuur zijn nobel bedrijf uitoefent, hebben geconstateerd, dat gemelde hond een zoogenaamde Schlemiel was. Gelijk bekend is de Schlemiel een Mischling met sterk-Semitische trekken. Het behoeft geen betoog, dat hieruit afleider blijkt, hoezeer de Joden ondanks alle zachte vermaningen en goed-bedoelde waarschuwingen van Duitsche zijde, hun duister bedrijf voortzetten. Men neemt in S.S.-kringen dan als vaststaand aan, dat de hond is afgericht op het wateren tegen Mauermuren.

Het tweede geval is er een van ergerlijk vandalisme, gepaard met beschadiging van voor de Weermacht belangrijke installaties. Op 16 Mei is een woerd door de tankgracht gezwommen en heeft met

zijn snavel een steen losgewrikt uit de bemanteling aan de binnenzijde. Daardoor is gevaar voor verzakking ontstaan. Door het onmiddellijk en heldhaftig optreden van een Duitschen militair die zich vergezeld van een Ehrenbraut in de nabijheid ophield, is erger voorkomen.

Het signalement van den dader luidt: Bruin colbertcostuum met een slobberhoed, sterk gebogen neus, wagnelende gang. Is hoogstwaarschijnlijk in het bezit van een Persoonsbewijs, waarvan de J langs chemischen weg is verwijderd. In verband met deze beide aanslagen op de eer en de veiligheid van de Duitsche Weermacht, stel ik de volgende straffen vast:

1. Het sluitingsuur van alle hondenasyls, hondenhokken, eendenkooien en daarmede gelijk te stellen instellingen te Haarlem wordt vervroegd tot 20 u. Het uur waarop honden en eenden zich niet meer op den openbaren weg mogen bevinden, wordt vastgesteld op 21 u.

2. Deze maatregel geldt niet voor de honden van de N.S.B., noch voor de eendenkuikens van de N.J.S.

3. Alle Ausweize voor Duitsche honden en eenden blijven geldig.

4. De Wethoudershond Fikkie Cosse wordt belast met het samenstellen van een wachtlooperslijst. Voorloopig voor den tijd van vier weken zal wachtgeloopen worden bij alle Mauermuren, urinoirs, tankgrachten, Wehrmachtsheime, Duitsche Bureaux en andere gelegenheden waar viezigheid gedeponeerd pleegt te worden.

w.g. RAUTER.

DEUTSCHES THEATER
in den Niederlanden
„DIE RÄUBER"
van Friedrich von Schiller.

Reeds vanaf 15 Mei 1940 doorloopende voorstellingen! In de hoofdrollen de bekende komieken:

SIJS EN CHRISTIAAN!

MAX BLOKZIJL
levert prima Duitsche Kulkoek

The Haarlemsche Courant—*the altered Haarlem newspaper—on June 5, 1944. (Courtesy of the author)* hiding places for them, transported them to safer places, and provided them with food stamps and other necessities. This was the group I belonged to for about one year.

Others took care of communications with England through radio transmissions, and within our country with the help of couriers who were riding their bicycles throughout Holland.

One group of underground workers, experts in printing, invaded the offices of the Haarlem *Daily News* late one night. They replaced the next day's completely printed edition full of German propaganda with, in the same format, the *Haarlem Newspaper*. The altered paper included articles about what really was taking place in our occupied country—about hunger, the treatment of political prisoners, and German atrocities. Nobody suspected a thing, and the *Haarlem Newspaper* was delivered to everyone.

Some people worked on the coding and decoding of messages that were to be sent to, or received from, England. My own family housed two young, very well-trained men from England who had parachuted out of airplanes and landed in our country. They brought a radio transmitter with them and were in contact with England nearly every day. Our house in Zaandam had a room on the third story with a window overlooking the busy street. One of the men stayed in that room, looking from behind the curtains to see if the coast was clear. The other man transmitted and received messages in a room at the back of the house. The messages were, of course, top secret.

One of my father's jobs was to code and decode those messages and deliver them to other members of the underground forces in our town. One day, with an extremely important message in his pocket, he knocked on the door of a house where underground activities had been taking place.

Two German officers opened the door—somehow they had found out about this house. My father, fluent in seven languages (Latin, Greek, Hebrew, French, English, German, and

Dutch), quickly started an amiable conversation with the German officers, telling them how he had tried and tried to get the owners of the house to come to church, but had not been successful so far. The Germans became very sympathetic and they talked religion with my father for quite a while. After a firm handshake, my father left with a smile, then rushed home, totally shaken. The owners of the house were shot to death some days later by the Germans, who had found out that those persons were involved in the group communicating with England through radio transmissions.

$-\phi-$

I did not know about my father's activities at the time, and he had no idea that I was involved in the Resistance, too. Those were things that were not discussed. After the war ended, my father told me about the message that nearly had fallen into the hands of the Germans: The young man in our upstairs room had received a warning from England that the large Dutch airport Schiphol would possibly be bombed by the Allied forces, and that the Resistance groups were to be warned in advance in order to save lives. The airport was used only by the Germans—no other planes were able to fly in or out.

22

FRIDAY MORNING

Every Friday morning at nine o'clock, the most important meeting of the Resistance was held somewhere in Amsterdam. To find a safe meeting place at a different location each week was sometimes very hard. It had to be an unobtrusive spot, a place that was humble, such as a room behind a little grocery store, a basement underneath a laundry business, or a classroom in an abandoned private school. The location had to be owned by somebody I knew and trusted, or by someone recommended to me by an underground worker I knew. And the owner of the building must never know what kind of meeting was to take place.

Of course, the Dutch had learned not to ask questions anymore, and in general, when asked to have the use of a room for a meeting, they obliged. They were reimbursed for the use and did not mind.

Nine gentlemen met every Friday morning in Amsterdam. Those nine were the leaders of all the different Resistance organizations in Holland. Each week they coordinated their plans and actions. Mr. van Tuyl was the leader. He was called "the Oilman," because he kept everything running smoothly.

During those meetings, both daily and future plans and actions were discussed. But the most important item of discussion was the planning of Holland's future after the war, which was worked out in great detail.

I was busy providing something to eat for the men or trying to keep the place a little bit warm with some coals, and all those very important events and plans usually went in one ear and out the other. For the safety of ourselves and our country, it was vitally important that we know as little as possible about what was going on. Should we be taken captive and tortured, there would be less information to be revealed.

I do remember, though, discussions of problems in connection with the railroad strike of September 1944. It was an impressive feat to organize the 30,000 people who worked for the railroad system. Many helpers were needed to distribute money and imitation coupons. But with the verbal and monetary support of the Dutch government in London, the whole plan worked out without a single flaw.

I still think of those nine men. One (I don't recall his name, which of course was not his real name anyway) I remember very clearly—a tall, charming, very well-dressed and handsome man, who always had time for some small conversation with me. I was rather shy, and he made me feel at ease. He asked me what kinds of things I liked to do in my free time. I told him that I longed to see American and English movies. No movies were shown during the war except for films full of German propaganda.[5]

There was a very quiet man, Mr. Dykstra, who eventually survived the war and became governor of Indonesia—which at that time still was a colony of Holland. There was also Mr. Buys, who I found out later had me followed and investigated for six weeks before I was given my new job as courier. And then, of course, there was Mr. van Tuyl.

23

RIDING THE BICYCLE

One morning at eight-thirty I had to meet a gentleman in the vaults of the large bank of Amsterdam. I went down numerous flights of marble stairs and found my way through dark corridors to my destination, where I met Mr. van Dyk (not his real name).

Mr. van Dyk handed me a package he had just taken out of the vault—a package the size and shape of a loaf of dark pumpernickel bread—and told me where it had to be delivered. He cautioned me and said, "Please be very careful with this package. It contains five million Dutch guilders [worth about three million U.S. dollars in 1944], and it is extremely important that it goes to the right person so he can have it distributed to several underground organizations in eastern Holland. Good luck with you and have a safe trip."

I gasped and swallowed, then answered Mr. van Dyk, "I will take good care of it." I had to deliver this package to an address in the town of Zwolle, in the eastern part of Holland, about one hundred kilometers from Amsterdam.

DER REICHSKOMMISSAR
FÜR DIE BESETZTEN NIEDERLÄNDISCHEN GEBIETE
DER BEAUFTRAGTE
FÜR DIE STADT AMSTERDAM

-Polizeioffizier-

AMSTERDAM, den 29.9.1944.
MUSEUMPLEIN 19
TEL. 97101

Nr. 306

B e s c h e i n i g u n g

Das Fahrrad Nr. 3728100.........Marke ..Fongers.............

des ...A.H. Eikema, D 29/Nr. 052155........................

wird zur Erreichung des Arbeitsplatzes benötigt. Von einer

Beschlagnahme ist abzusehen.

One of these permits was needed when riding a bicycle. The bottom one is genuine, issued by the Germans. The top one is falsified. (Courtesy of the author)

Der Beauftragte des Reichskommissars
für die Stadt Amsterdam
— Polizeioffizier —

GÜLTIG BIS 10.12.1944.

AMSTERDAM, 25. 10.1944.

B E S C H E I N I G U N G Nr. 1842

Das Fahrrad Nr. ...3.728.100........ Marke ..Fongers...

des A.H. Eikema, Noorder Amstellaan 63 I, Amsterdam

wird zu beruflichen Zwecken dringend benötigt. Von

einer Beschlagnahme ist abzusehen.

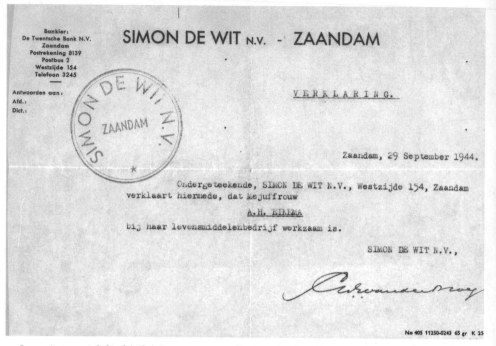

I sometimes carried this falsified document, stating that I worked for a chain of grocery stores, in case I was stopped by the Germans. (Courtesy of the author)

Everybody in the Resistance had learned that if you had something valuable to transport, it was best not to hide it but to carry it openly. It was a small trick told to novice workers by more experienced Resistance members. I put the package along with a sandwich, an apple, and my hideous imitation cigarettes in the small basket hanging from the handlebars of my bike.

I started out. Ten-speed or even three-speed bicycles did not exist. We rode only heavy bikes, which were hard to pedal. And, as always, the everlasting wind was blowing against me on that flat land.

The trip progressed slowly, since the wind was strong. At the rate I was going it was doubtful that I would reach the east side of Holland by curfew time. The only traffic on the road was German trucks. Nobody else had any means of motorized transportation.

Suddenly a large, open German truck passed and slowed down a bit. I grabbed a rail on the back of the truck and wheeled behind it at great speed. The German driver waved occasionally at me, and I smiled back broadly. After two hours of free wheeling, I let go very close to my destination. My hands were cramped and cold, but I found the address in Zwolle before curfew and delivered the five million guilders.

24

THE BATTLE OF ARNHEM

The tragic battle of Arnhem took place in September 1944. The Allied forces, in their attempt to return freedom from the occupying Germans to all of Holland, were defeated, and many lives were lost.

The southern part of Holland, below the river Rhine, which flowed calmly through the lowlands of both the north and the south, was liberated by the Allies. The northern part of Holland remained occupied by the Germans, causing this part to go through another winter of suffering. Sixteen thousand Dutch men, women, and children died of cold and hunger.

25

The "Hunger Winter," 1944–1945

About once a month I traveled home from Amsterdam. Each time I arrived at our house, I found that the food situation had become worse. My family had a little bit of grain, a gift from a farmer. Every day some of this grain was ground up in our small coffee grinder. It was mixed with water and fried in a frying pan with a small teaspoon of lard. For many days that was my family's dinner.

We ate toothpaste, which was still available, and tulip bulbs. In some restaurants the only item on the menu was baked dog.

In Amsterdam it was slightly better for us. Some of the Resistance workers occasionally stole food from German warehouses and gave those who worked for the NSF some of this food. The loot consisted mostly of canned German Army rations, which looked and tasted like a poor quality dog food, or canned, mashed carrots, which were tasteless but filled you up some. A pack of cigarettes was often added, which was greatly appreciated—and a welcome change after having collected cigarette butts from the gutters and rolled tobacco from these butts to make cigarettes. I became very good at this and could roll a cigarette with one hand.

Many Dutch people rode their bicycles to the northern parts of Holland to find food. Farmers in the country always shared what they had. It was not much, because it had to be divided among so many, but even

Some bicycles were in such poor condition that they could not survive the difficult journey back from the countryside, where their owners had ventured in search of food. (Courtesy of the author)

the smallest gift was gladly and gratefully accepted.

The bicycles had wooden wheels, as rubber tires had worn out, and new rubber tires were very hard to come by. In this cold winter the roads were icy, but the hungry men and women moved on slowly, hour after hour. They had to cross a bridge over a river to bring them to the northeast, where many farmers lived. They had tied burlap sacks and baskets to their bicycles, which they hoped to fill with potatoes, cabbages, and other produce, if they were lucky enough to find farmers who still had some stashed away.

On their last trip they found the bridge closed. The Allies had captured the bridge. They did not allow anyone to cross this new border, as security was tight and there was always the possibility of spies traveling from Germany to Holland. The food searchers had to turn back, without hope, without any food to take back to their families, and many died along the roads, on the long way home.

26

THE LOST BICYCLE

The Leidsche Gracht in Amsterdam, 1991, where one underground group leader rode into the canal on a foggy night in 1944. (Photograph by Fred Hager)

Much happened in the houses along the canals in Amsterdam. One of the busiest streets seemed to be the Leidsche Gracht. Many meetings were held there in the different houses. All of us came on bicycles, which we parked inside, to prevent them from being stolen. When a meeting room happened to be upstairs, we had to carry our bikes up flights of stairs, an awkward and tedious task.

One dark and foggy winter afternoon, one of the underground group leaders came bicycling to a Leidsche Gracht meeting place. He misjudged the narrow road in the fog and the dark and ended up in the canal. Fortunately, he was able to climb out of the water, but his bicycle disappeared. He had pockets full of very important papers, and they were all soaked. The whole meeting room was suddenly covered with documents that had to dry as soon as possible, without noise and by candlelight.

27

A New Fight, January 1945

Lots of us who were working in the Resistance switched from living place to living place during the last months of the war in case we were followed by the German SS.

It was Friday morning and the cold crept through the walls, the windows, and the doors of the stately old house along one of Amsterdam's canals.

There were five of us staying in this large house: van Tuyl, his assistant Brinkie, one young member of a sabotage group by the name of Wim, a courier called Ankie, and me.

We did not feel the cold, though, as we had pulled out the little radio from its hiding place behind a cupboard in the kitchen, and all of us were totally absorbed in what was broadcast from England that morning: Winston Churchill was delivering one of his famous speeches; he was growling, he was howling, he was touching our hearts and giving us hope. His words vibrated through the cold and drafty room. I still remember one of his first speeches at the beginning of the war in 1940: "And we will never surrender." Those words echoed in my head every time we listened to him.[6]

We put the radio carefully away in its hiding place; it was time to go to the Friday morning meeting. Van Tuyl was to leave the house first and head to the place designated for this morning, again an old brick building along another canal in Amsterdam. His last words before he left were, "Do not ever let on that you know van Tuyl. The Germans have been looking for me for a long time now. Good-bye and see you soon." And then he left, tired and bent over, wrapped in a worn-out winter coat, but with a gleam in his eyes and a heart full of love and compassion.

I followed a few minutes later, arms full of brussels sprouts, some old toasted bread, and a small sack of coals. The ten-minute walk was invigorating; it felt good to be outside under the cold, blue sky, thinking about Winston Churchill's words, realizing how good he made us feel and how proud.

The house on the Leidsche Gracht, where we were arrested. I went up the outside steps and through the front door, where the Germans were waiting. They took me up to the second story and that is where the five leaders were lying on the floor. These photographs were taken when I returned to the Netherlands with my husband in 1986. (Courtesy of the author)

—✦—

The moment I walked into the meetinghouse, two very large Germans with machine guns jumped at me, screaming at me to drop everything I was holding in my arms. The brussels sprouts scattered all over the floor and so did the coals from the little sack. One of the Germans tripped over a coal and uttered a loud curse.

They escorted me upstairs, a gun pointed in my back. When I entered the upstairs room, I saw five men lying facedown on the floor, hands above their heads. Van Tuyl was one of them. The Germans offered me a chair and a cigarette. I accepted the cigarette and started to smoke and acted as casual as I possibly could.

No words were spoken to any of the men on the floor or to me. The silence was eerie; it felt as if we were waiting to be tortured, or waiting to die. One of the men on the floor was moaning softly, the others were very quiet.

After about ten minutes, German reinforcements arrived, and two heavily armed German officers took me out of the room. That was the last I saw of my boss, van Tuyl, and of some of the other gentlemen of the Friday morning meetings.

The prison, 1986. (Photograph by Les Ippisch)

I was pushed down the stairs and into the backseat of a waiting car. One of the Germans sat on one side of me, the other one on the other side, and a third German was the driver. We drove through Amsterdam and arrived at the big prison. In the front office, close to the entry door, I was told to strip completely and hand over my watch and purse. My clothes were thoroughly searched before I was allowed to put them on again; then I was taken to D12—my cell, a space of about five feet by eight feet. In this cell were four women, bunk beds with some blankets, a small table, two stools, and a bucket that was used as a toilet.

Often the first reaction for a new prisoner is to walk back and forth in the cell, back and forth for a long time. I guess it is an impulse to get acquainted with the new territory. The next impulse is to unburden yourself— to talk about everything to anybody who will listen. We were warned about

The window in our cell, 1986. (Photograph by Les Ippisch)

this, though. Many times "a sympathetic listener" would be planted in a cell to repeat to the Germans what the new prisoner had said. Usually after a couple of days the "sympathetic cellmate" was released. So after the walking ended, one just kept silent.

If you wonder if I was afraid when I was arrested, I have to tell you that I was not. I was numb. My work in the Resistance had been stopped. I did not know for how long or if it was forever. And when the numbness ceased I became angry. I was helpless in this cell, unable to fight any longer for freedom. Little by little I began to realize that now a new fight had started, the fight for per-

sonal survival, the struggle to stay alert and strong, both mentally
and physically, and the struggle to become accustomed to the fact
that I was now a political prisoner at the age of nineteen.

Amsterdam, datum postmerk.

Ik bevind mij thans in de Duitse Afdeling van het Huis van Bewaring II,
Havenstraat no. 6, Amsterdam. — Ik verzoek U, mij op Vrijdag tussen
9—12 en 2—5 uur schoon wasgoed te willen sturen, goed verpakt in een
kussensloop en voorzien van mijn naam en celnummer. Levens- en Genot-
middelen mogen niet worden mede gegeven. Zeep, tandpasta en tanden-
borstel kan worden medegestuurd. Op Vrijdag kan het vuile wasgoed
worden afgehaald. *Correspondentie is verboden.*

Wasgoed brengen : Vrijdag om de 14 dagen.
„   halen : Vrijdag volgende op het brengen.

Eikema   Albertine
Naam en Voornamen.
Celnummer, D.2—12 2 -11

Het Huis van Bewaring is *niet* aansprakelijk voor weggeraakt wasgoed.

DE COMMANDANT.

The card sent to my parents when I was arrested, informing them that I was in prison. It tells them that they can send me clean laundry, soap, and toothpaste, but no food. "Albertine" is my first name, which I rarely used. My cell number was D2 (second floor), number 12. I don't know why the number was changed here. (Courtesy of the author)

28

SKY

The cell was very small indeed and did not offer comfort. It was cold and damp and hard and dark. It was not long before we were covered with lice, which thrived and became fat and healthy. But the cell became home for the four of us for several long months.

High up was a small window covered with thick iron bars. I could see the sky, that beautiful Dutch sky, always changing. There were times when it was a brilliant blue, but often the clouds sailed by, blown by the strong Dutch wind. Mostly, though, the sky was gray and full of sadness and the rain came down for days on end as if shedding tears for all of us who suffered.

29

BRICKS

There were bricks everywhere, except for the heavy cell door with the small peephole and the window high up, which gave us some daylight.

There were brick walls on all sides, rows upon rows of bricks, worn with age. Water was slowly dripping down, forming small streams, dripping from brick to brick, finding a way to the always wet cement floor. Some bricks glistened in the sparse light of a single lightbulb, which was hanging high from the ceiling. The bricks were full of small dents and cracks, which offered footholds for cockroaches who crawled straight up and disappeared into hiding places, and for mice who ran up and down, playing hide-and-seek, trying to find a crumb on the floor.

An occasional rat with a long shiny tail, seemingly coming from nowhere, climbed up through the crevices between the bricks and left a trail on the wet walls.

The prisoners before us had scratched their initials on

the bricks and had added marks, showing how many hours and days, weeks and months they had lived in this cell.

There were a few messages of hope:

Vrĳ nederland — Free Netherland
Lang leve de Koningen — Long live the Queen
Wy zullen winnen — We will conquer

And some were full of hate and despair:

Dood aan de rotmoffen — Death to the barbarians
Verraders zullen hangen — Traitors will hang
Laat voor my het einde spoedig komen — Please make the
    end come soon for me

> A cell is only four yards long
> And barely two yards wide.
> But smaller is the piece of ground
> Which will become the side
> For some of us to wait and stand
> So patient for the end.
>
> And when the time has come to die
> God show us to be brave
> And help us keep our heads up high
> So that the last we see will be
> The everchanging sky.[7]

30

OUR DAILY BREAD

Day started early in the prison in Amsterdam. At six o'clock in the morning we woke up to the sound of slamming doors, the rattling of tin dishes, and the hollering of commands in German. It was breakfast time. We could always tell when we would receive our breakfast—the sound of the heavy cell doors slamming came closer and finally our door was thrown open. One guard handed us our food while another watched and pointed his gun at us. We grabbed the tin plates and cups and handed over our overflowing toilet bucket.

Breakfast consisted of one cup of imitation coffee and one piece of bread, often moldy. But we learned to eat slowly, and we watched each other's crumbs. . . . If any fell on the floor, we were very quick to pick them up to stick them in our own mouths.

At noon the same procedure was repeated, but this time we got thin, watery soup, with an occasional slice of carrot or potato floating on top. Dinner was the same as lunch. We often talked about the elaborate meals we were going to indulge in when and if we were freed.

The food had an odd taste, but we did not know why. After the war we found out there always was a small portion of camphor put in all of our food to reduce our sexual desires and eventually prevent us from having monthly periods. If one was subject to this kind of adulterated food for a year or longer, one would become totally sterile.

We were constantly hungry. It's a feeling we learned to accept, a gnawing sensation that never left.

Once a week we were herded out of our cell for a shower and a walk in an outside cage, covered on all sides and top with wire. Sometimes the sun was shining, which warmed our bodies. Mostly it was cold, though, bitterly cold.

When we walked around and around in our outside cage, we always sang loud and clear, often French songs. We got into trouble for that numerous times. The Germans yelled at us to stop singing in English!

After the cold outside it actually felt good to come back to the "safety" of our cell. It was not much warmer than the outside, but there were four solid walls and a solid ceiling protecting us from the wind.

31

CELL MATES

There were four of us in this cell. The fifth one was released after two days, which convinced us that she had been planted in our cell as a sympathetic listener. She had said very little, but had tried to get answers from us to the questions she had asked.

Nel, twenty-two, was caught delivering underground newspapers. Tine, an older woman, had been busy making profits by black-marketing (stealing food and cigarettes and selling these items for high profits). Gerda, in her late twenties, was found digging a hole in her backyard in order to hide copper and brass antiques. Then there was me, nineteen.

We learned that Tine would be released soon, as her "crime" was not political and the Germans needed all the spaces in the cells for more prisoners. But Tine was sympathetic to our cause, our resistance to the Germans, and all four of us got along quite nicely. The trouble with Tine was that she was not well. She suffered from dysentery, and we were afraid to catch it from her, as the conditions were completely unsanitary. We all shared the toilet bucket, which was small and often overflowed.

My cell mates and I learned to pass the long days as best we could by singing songs, doing push-ups, walking back and forth, keeping the little place tidy, devising games, and dividing the days into segments—each segment designated for a certain chore, entertainment, or educational exercise.

Sometimes we sang the song of the American hoboes:

Why don't you go and work when there is so much to do?
How can we go and work when there is no work to do?
Hallelujah! I am a bum—bum!
Hallelujah! Bum again.
Hallelujah! Give us a handout
To revive us again.

This silly song went well when we were marching around in our cell.

At times we got totally carried away with the very sentimental French love songs:

J'attendrai le jour et la nuit,
j'attendrai toujour ton retour.
J'attendrai car l'oisseau qui s'enfuit
vient chercher l'oubli dans son nid.
Le temps passe en court en battant tristement
dans mon coeur plus lourd
Et pourtant j'attendrai ton retour.

Freely translated:

I will wait day and night,
I will always wait for your return.
I will wait because the bird who has flown away
Will come back to his nest to look for the things he forgot.
The time is passing in my very heavy heart
However I will always wait for your return.[8]

At night, when the small lightbulb hanging from the ceiling went out, we always sang softly the Dutch words to the melody of "Taps." Translated, the words of this melody are:

Day is done
Gone the sun
· From the sea
From the land
From the sky.
All is well
Safely rest
God is nigh.

Dag gedaan.
Zon verdwynd.
Van de lucht.
Van het land
Van de zee.
Alles goed, slaap in vree.
God is hier.[9]

32

THE MAIL

After about six weeks we found a way to establish some contact with the outside world. We had ample time, and we became very good at writing miniature letters on toilet paper. We did not have a pencil at first, so I wrote my first letter with a broken-off fingernail. I carefully etched letter after letter on a piece of toilet paper approximately three quarters of an inch by one half an inch. After finishing this letter, I folded it several times until it was about one-quarter-inch square.

My family was informed by an underground worker that it would be a good idea to try to insert a pencil and a sewing needle in a small tube of toothpaste, which could be included in the sack of laundry to be delivered to the prison. As we sometimes received laundry, there would be a chance that we would find these very valuable items. And, indeed, we found both a needle and a pencil.

We opened up the laundry marks* on our clothing and

* Laundry marks were less than one inch in size and were always sewn on our clothing at the back of the neck. They had our initials, in my case "H. E.," embroidered on thin white cotton. Laundry marks helped to identify the owners of clothing.

My laundry marks. H. E. stands for Hanneke Eikema, my maiden name. (Courtesy of the author)

One laundry mark.

One folded laundry mark, sewn on clothing.

inserted our letters. As we were the lucky owners of a needle, we were able to sew the laundry mark closed again. All incoming and outgoing laundry was X-rayed, but the small, hidden letters were never detected.

The underground worker also told my family to look for news from me in the dirty laundry they were to pick up from the prison in Amsterdam. They quickly caught on and sent me small letters from home, hidden behind those laundry marks. I swallowed those little letters immediately after reading them. But my family kept the letters I sent them and they are still readable after all those years.

My family went through great efforts and agony to receive these signs of life. First, my father or my sister rode approximately thirty miles to Amsterdam on a bicycle with wooden wheels to get my dirty laundry, which was released only if the guards were in a good mood. Then came the trip home from Amsterdam and the desperate attempt to be home before dark and curfew. There was no electricity anymore, there were no streetlights, and the only light inside at night came from a small wick floating in oil in a saucer. The search for news started by this light and my family examined all the clothing to see if there were any letters from me.

Letters written while in prison, which my family kept. (Photograph by Steve Pike)

Here is a partial translation of letter number nine, seen here second to top, resting on the middle finger. V. is short for Vader (*"Father"*). We did not use complete names because it was not safe to do so.

"News received from V. We long very much to get clean laundry. That is something we are so looking forward to. The last days we did not get food or water. We had laughed out loud in our cell, which they heard!"

Here are more translations of small letters sent out of prison:

Dearest V. M. L., {Vader, Moeder, Lied. ("Father," "Mother," "Lied.")}
Really lucked out! The forty-five most "dangerous" women were to be sent to Germany. At the very last minute it did not happen.[10] *Send next time more letters. Many possibilities for small notes and I have time to send more myself.*

Dearest V., Many warm congratulations on your birthday. A birthday hug you will receive when the fatted calf is butchered upon the arrival of the "lost daughter." Unfortunately I think we are getting no more letters inside the prison. My birthday celebrated with sick, vomiting "black market" woman and two nice others. Letter of 3/16 received and all notes of 3/23, what fun. Write in the future with ink, please. {Next sentence not discernable.}
Hugs, Hanneke.

33

THE SNOWDROP

The gloominess of the cell started to affect us after about two months. I was desperate for something new to look at, something that proved that outside there was life and new growth. I wanted to know that in spite of all the misery of the war, there were flowers in beautiful colors, blooming to announce the arrival of spring.

I sent a small letter to my family and asked them to hide a little snowdrop, the earliest blooming spring flower, in my clean laundry. I never did receive it. However, thinking about it and hoping that the small flower would come to cheer us made us feel better.

Long after the war, my sister told me she had indeed sent a little snowdrop to me, hidden in a sock in my clean laundry. She had always wondered if I had found that sign of spring.

34

A Letter from My Father
to Our Relatives

February 10, 1945

Dear Family!

Yesterday we received T.'s letter sent January 4th. Finally some progress in the mail delivery. For a long time it was hopeless. We heard in that letter that Grandmother had been home from the hospital for a week and that all is well with her.

S. does all right. She gets out of bed every day for about an hour, to walk, as the doctor asked her to do.

Yesterday L. and I went to the prison in Amsterdam to bring clean laundry to H. In the pillowcase with clean laundry we put some slices of the delicious Swedish bread that the Swedish Red Cross had sent, but the bread was confiscated immediately.

Of course we did not get to talk to her, but I spoke a few words with a German guard, who told me that both treatment and food were excellent (!!!!), and that all women and girls were very cheerful (!!!!!).

H. is in the part of the building where all female political prisoners are kept. Next week, Friday, we will be able to pick up her dirty laundry. Also, I have to tell you that cousin B. in Groningen is in prison, too!

We have new hope that the war here in the west soon will be over, and that all the misery will end.

Yesterday morning, just when we were leaving Amsterdam on our bicycles, there was suddenly a crowd running and bicycling, trying to escape to the north, while shouting, "Razzia, Razzia" {a slang word for warning and to be alert}. The "Greens" {Germans} had arrived and shot ten young men to death in the center of Amsterdam. I believe they were partisans from the northern part of Holland. Also in Amsterdam, five very well-known men were shot to death two days ago; William D., the president of our church organization in Holland, was one of them. You might remember him—a noble man. I talked to him often when I gave sermons in Amsterdam. What a world! But—we keep courage!

When I go back to Amsterdam, I have to try to get wooden wheels for my bicycle. I can hardly use my old tires anymore; they are nearly worn out.

It is wonderful that Spring is arriving. Daughter L. went on her bicycle to Schagen. The trip took her two days. She had quite good weather, but there is not much food to get there either. However, she did come home with a small piece of pork and some brussels sprouts, given to her by our former maid, G., who had married a farmer. The day before yesterday, one of our members of the church in Dordrecht, who owns a small grocery store, stopped by and presented us with a small package of tea and some sugar cubes. That same day an unknown person delivered us a bucket of coal. Last week, a relative of an old person, whose funeral I took care of, presented us with a whole pound of cooking pears. We did enjoy them so much.

From H. we do not hear anything. I'm sure she'll have her birthday in prison.

But in spite of it all, we remain optimistic.

Many warm greetings,
J.[11]

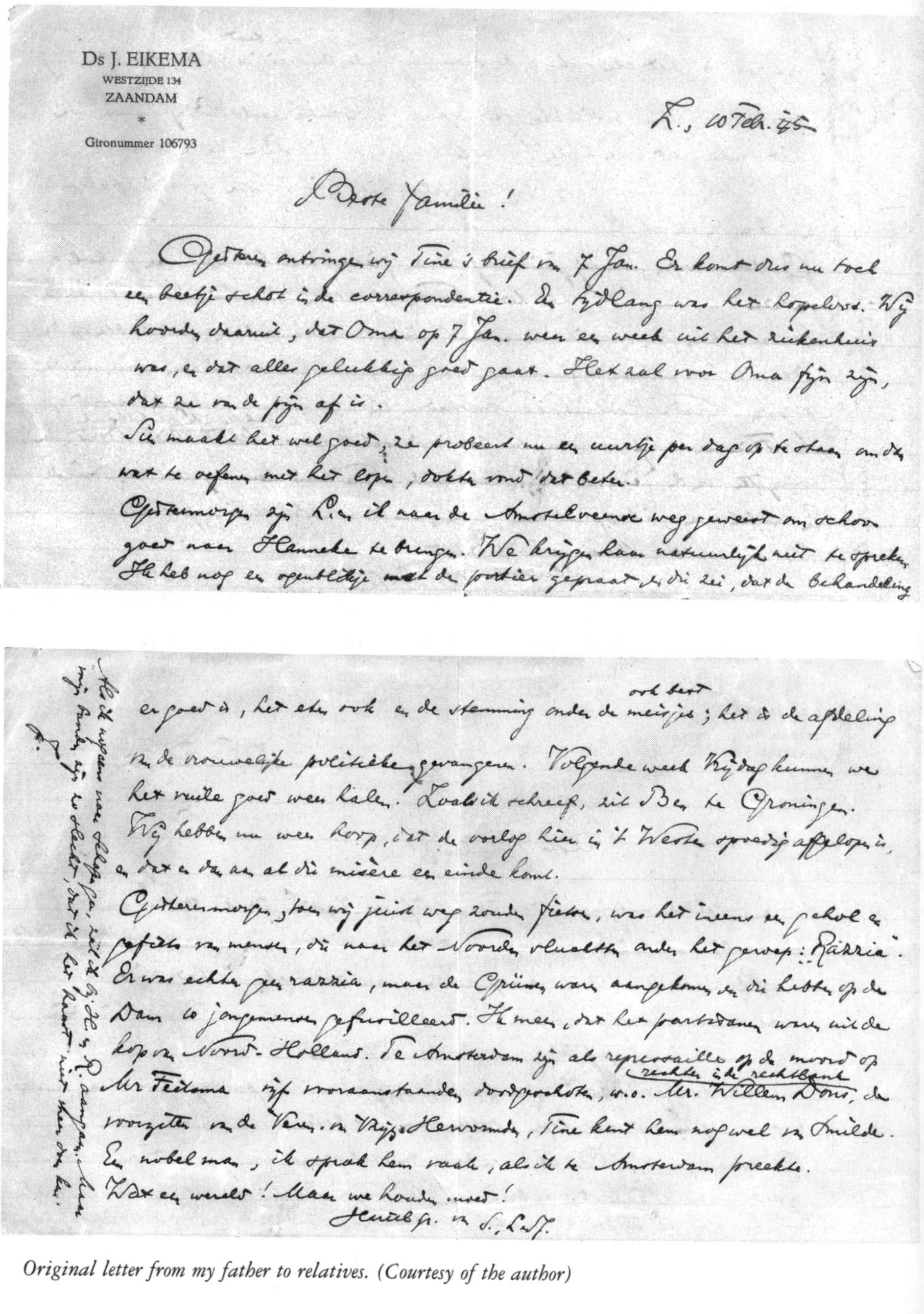

Ds J. EIKEMA
WESTZIJDE 134
ZAANDAM
*
Gironummer 106793

Z., 10 Feb. '45

Beste Familie!

[handwritten letter in Dutch]

Original letter from my father to relatives. (Courtesy of the author)

35

THE INTERROGATION

The cell door opened. All four of us had dreaded this moment, and not one of us knew what was to happen. A German guard, holding a gun, grabbed my arm and took me outside the cell.

"Kommen Sie schnell bitte" ("Come quick please"), he said. He ushered me down metal stairways, through corridors with thick iron doors, one more stairway up, and then he knocked on a door. The door was opened by another guard. We entered a roomy office with a large desk.

Behind the desk sat a German officer whose name, I was told, was Ruhl. I had to sit on a chair next to him. At his feet were two huge Dobermans, and when I sat down they got up and both started to sniff menacingly at me. Then they retreated to their master.

Ruhl threw a photo at me. *"Wem ist das?"* ("Who is this?") he said. I pretended not to understand him, and shrugged my shoulders. *"Wem ist das? Ich weis das Sie den man gesehen haben."* ("Who is that? I know that you have seen this man.") I recognized the man in the photo. It was Hugo, one of the members of the Friday morning meetings.

The German officer, Ruhl, continued in German: "I know that you know him. He was arrested before you and your friends were caught. He told us all about you and the others. There is no point in denying it. It would be a lot smarter to cooperate." He softly whistled, and the dogs stood up and showed their teeth.

"I have seen that man, maybe once. I do not know him, and I do not know his name," I answered. Impatiently Ruhl shook his head and softly whistled again. The dogs came closer to me.

"You must cooperate," Ruhl said, irritated.

"Okay," I answered. "I belong to a rowing and sailing organization in Zaandam of which many people are members. Sometimes some of the members meet between office hours and discuss the rowing and sailing events that are coming up. Since I study in Amsterdam, they ask me to bring them some food and some coals to warm their meeting place. They pay me a little money, one Dutch guilder and fifty cents, to be exact, which helps me to pay the rent for my room."

Ruhl shifted in his chair, growing more impatient. "I know that you know these men very well and that you were helping them. We looked for them for four years, until we arrested them recently. It would be so much better for you, such a young and pretty girl, to tell me what you really know. We would hate to harm you; you can have a long life ahead of you yet."

"I told you what I know," I answered. "I'm very sorry, but that is all I know. I wish I could help you more, but I simply can't." I tried to cry, to appear sad and innocent, but could not. My tears were gone.

Ruhl whistled a little louder. The dogs now started to growl and began to sniff my legs and skirt, and Ruhl kept asking the same questions. I gave him the same answers as before.

This went on for four hours. Ruhl ordered a lunch

consisting of Swedish bread, cheese, and coffee, which he ate slowly and loudly, smacking his mouth repeatedly. I looked at his food and my stomach hurt from hunger.

He rang a small bell and another German officer entered. The two of them started to talk and had some more food brought in and some more coffee. This time they also devoured large pieces of greasy-looking German sausages. My stomach was growling and hurt even more.

Ruhl fed the dogs the leftovers of his lunch and began to ask me the same questions as before. I answered in the same way as before. Over and over he repeated the same questions; over and over I gave him the same answers.

Suddenly Ruhl became disgusted. He rang for a guard and ordered me back to the cell. Quite shaken but also very relieved that this first interrogation was behind me, I returned to the relative safety of our cell.

Every day and every night we expected the door to open again, but it never did. We concluded that the Germans were too busy preparing for the end of the war. They had to decide which safety precautions they could take for themselves, because even they could see that their German victories were over, and that the end was very near.

36

THE DUNGEON

We often got world news from the occupants of the cell on the floor below. They were thieves and murderers and they had certain privileges, including newspapers. Political prisoners were not allowed to receive newspapers.

The prisoners below sympathized with the political prisoners and regularly hollered the latest news through the drainpipes, which ran vertically outside from floor to floor.

They told us there was hardly anything to eat in Holland. People died by the hundreds along the roads. It was too cold—this last winter of the war—too cold to dig graves. So the bodies were piled up high in the churches.

Sweden, a neutral country, did many good things during that last winter. The Swedish Red Cross sent bread and margarine for all the people in Holland, including the prisoners. Much bread was delivered to our prison in Amsterdam and was placed in front of our cell doors. We smelled it often, but we never saw any of it. The German guards must have eaten it all.

One day, on April 19, we learned from the floor below us that the beautiful old town of Vienna, in Austria, had been bombed by the Allied forces. We also heard that President Roosevelt had died in the United States. The next few words of news made us very excited. It looked as if the war's end was in sight.

The entrance to our cell, D12, in 1986. (Photograph by Les Ippisch)

It was my turn to pass the news to the next level above us, to the male political prisoners. I stepped on the little stool by the cell window and started to shout the news up through the drainpipe. Suddenly, I had the strange feeling that something was behind me. I jumped down, turned around, and saw a glistening eye staring through the small peephole in the thick cell door. The door was thrown open, and a raving mad German prison commander grabbed me and transported me to "the dungeon"—a cell in the basement of the prison. The dungeon was without light, without heat, and without a blanket, bed, or food. I stayed in this cell for five days, practicing ballet steps to keep warm.

When I became too hungry and too cold, I hunched up and started to dream. I dreamt about the times when I was small and safe with parents who took care of me, and an older sister to look after me and to argue with me, and with a maid who saw to it that meals were cooked on time.

I dreamt about Sundays in the small village I lived in. On Sunday mornings

Our cell, 1986. (Photograph by Les Ippisch)

My father in his toga, 1947. (Courtesy of the author)

my father walked the pathway from our house to the church. He always wore a long black toga and a snowy white bib crackling with starch. On his head he had a black velvet beret that I often stroked because it was so soft. He had a majestic voice, and when he sang the hymns with the people in the church I sometimes closed my eyes to listen to the voice of my father.

The church bells rang loud and clear as we walked to the church. It was the job of the church caretaker to ring the bell each Sunday morning. Sometimes I was allowed to help him pull the rope down. If I did not let go, the rope pulled me up in the air several feet, but it felt as if I were flying in the sky.

I woke up to the sound of heavy footsteps going past my cell and I shivered. There was a small crack under my door throwing some light, and each time I heard footsteps go by, there was a shadow cast over this little line of light. I kept quiet and listened to the sound of footsteps slowly disappearing. I crouched together again.

When I was seven years old I moved with my family to the small town of Schagen in western Holland. Ministers moved rather often in those days because they felt that a congregation would get tired of the same sermons and it was always healthy to see a new face in the pulpit. Each move meant a larger and better job for the minister, a job subsidized by the government of Holland.

Our house, the parsonage, was on a quiet street bordered by a

My father, mother, sister, and me in 1928. I am next to my mother. (Courtesy of the author)

The arched footbridge my sister and I walked across to get to school. Lied and I (left) are standing near the middle of the bridge in this 1938 picture. (Photograph by Jan Eikema)

canal with a round arched footbridge spanning the water. Every day I walked with my older sister over the arched bridge to go to school, and every day I walked back over the arched bridge with my sister to go home.

One day I got an uncontrollable urge to conquer the water. When the weather was clear and all the people were in their homes to eat supper, I stole away from my house and climbed into a rowboat moored to a small pier.

The little boat rocked and rolled until I got my balance; I grabbed the oars and started rowing. Awkward at first, I splashed water all around me. But after a while I learned to control the boat somewhat, and actually moved along quite nicely. I was concentrating on the mastering of my surroundings when I realized that a lot of shouting and yelling was going on. I looked up and suddenly saw people on the arched bridge, waving arms and fists and shouting. In the middle of them was my father. As they hollered and yelled at me to come home, I became so frightened of the punishment waiting for me that I kept rowing in circles, careful not to come too close to shore. I kept rowing and rowing, conquering the seven seas.

+

Perhaps night had arrived, as I did not see the small line of light anymore. The cold, the hunger, and the thirst were keeping me awake. I heard a vague noise and I realized that it was the gentle drip of water coming from somewhere. Carefully I started to feel the brick walls in the dark with my hands. I seemed to come closer to the sound and then felt water on my arm. I held my hand under the small drip and was able to collect several drops of water, which quenched my thirst, and I fell asleep.

I woke up when the small line of light showed underneath the cell door again. I smiled, thinking about the time when I felt I needed to be prepared. Twice a month our seamstress came to our house to alter our clothes or to make new outfits for my sister and me. When she was making skirts, I always begged her to sew deep, large pockets in the side seams so that I could store all the things I thought I needed to have with me, and the nice seamstress did just that.

From then on I was prepared! My pockets were stuffed full with necessities such as a compass, a first aid kit, a notebook and pencil, and a bandanna to tie around a broken arm or leg. I always wore my father's old leather belt from which I proudly hung a pocketknife and a rope to save people if they were drowning. The rope was only three feet long, but I never thought of that.

+

One day I secretly left home on my bike. I pedaled forever, it seemed, and as the sun was high in the sky and the heat of the day made everything simmer, I stopped by some shrubbery along the road. I heard a noise inside a shrub and when I looked I noticed a bird caught in the branches. Carefully I lifted the bird out of the thicket and put a Band-Aid on one of his legs. Then I let it go. How proud I was of this rescue!

I decided to bicycle home, having visions of very worried parents waiting outside, hoping for a sign of life from me. When I reached home, all was normal and quiet, and I found that nobody had even missed me. The time span from my departure to return covered in reality only twenty-five minutes. For me it seemed that many hours had passed.

After four days in the dark cell I started to become very tired and listless. I could still collect water, though, a little at a time, and this helped me not to become dehydrated, and when the fifth morning arrived and the small line of light again showed below the cell door, it felt as if the sun was shining.

—♦—

When winter arrived in Holland, when all the canals froze over, the schools closed and everyone went skating. The teachers and the students—all of us were on the ice with our long wooden skates. It was not every year that all the smaller and larger canals, the lakes, and the inland seas froze to make good skating ice, so when it happened, it was practically a national holiday.

We did not practice figure skating. It was the distance

A wooden skate. (Photograph by Steve Pike)

skating we all loved so much. We were half bent over, arms on backs, battling the wind, taking long strides and traveling long distances along the dikes, past small villages and windmills.

Often trips were organized. We started out very early in the morning once dawn had come to help us see the ice. We skated from windmill to windmill, and at each mill we received a stamp on our card. It was a windmill skating race. If you managed to skate by all the mills along the designated route in one day, you were awarded a medal.

We skated all day. At several places small stalls were set up and covered with tarps. Benches were placed inside the stalls on the ice, and pea soup with sausages, and chocolate were kept piping hot on woodstoves.

After a short break we went on to try to reach our destination before the sun set. Sometimes we hitched a ride by lashing on to some tough and strong men who skated so fast, they flew like seagulls, barely touching the ice. They tied their wooden skates right to their feet with cotton straps and did not need boots at all. The only protection they had from the cold was their thick black wool socks.

I was awarded this medal for completing the windmill ice skating trip in 1941. (Courtesy of the author)

There were many older people who skated, often in pairs; he with a pipe in his mouth, she with a kerchief tied around her head to protect her ears from the cold wind, and a long skirt with a checkered apron, apron strings fluttering behind her back.

There were whole families, father in front with a broomstick, and the mother and children holding on to it. Together they skated in unison, right leg, left leg, right leg, left leg— the rhythm never changed. On and on the families went toward the horizon.

The wings of the windmills, turned by the wind, saluted all of the skaters in Holland, and the only sounds were the cutting on the ice from the steel on the bottom of the wooden skates, the occasional mooing of a cow, and the clear, high ringing of a church bell far away.

I did make it by sunset once, skating past all the mills before dark, and the medal I won is one of the treasures I look at sometimes and smile.

—◦—

After five days the cell door was opened. A German officer hollered: *"Aus Steigen bitte!"* ("Get out please!")

I got off the floor and was escorted along the stairways, past the long rows of heavy cell doors, back to D12, my cell. Once inside I sighed with relief.

My cell mate Gerda took something from underneath the mattress and handed it to me with a smile. "Here is a piece of bread from all three of us. It was not easy to save it, but we hoped that you would come back."

37

Out at Last

A week before the war officially ended, the Germans had to sign papers promising to release the political prisoners in Holland. A few days prior to this we had been transported to a large assembly room in the prison, where about eighty of us spent our last days in captivity. It was wonderful to see some old friends again, and we talked for many hours about all that had happened. There was a large bucket of potatoes in the big room, and many of us who had been in prison for a longer time ate them raw and actually enjoyed them, as we were so very, very hungry.

The Germans set us free a few at a time. When my turn came, I was escorted to a large meeting room with seven high-ranking Germans sitting behind a conference table covered with a green felt cloth. One of them gave me a long speech about the horrible mistakes we had made by working against the Germans. I had to promise to never get involved in illegal activities again. Then they opened the locked doors and the big gates, and I suddenly stood in a street outside the prison in Amsterdam, shaggy, dirty, and carrying a pillowcase full of soiled clothes on my back.

I felt numb and weak, but wanted to get away from there. I tried to find a phone, but phones were disconnected and Amsterdam seemed totally deserted. So, I started to walk the long way home. I trudged slowly; a few German trucks passed me. I heard the rattling of a bicycle with wooden wheels behind me and I turned around. To my great joy I saw an old Girl Scout friend of mine who lived in the same town as my family.

"Hello there, Hanneke," she said, amazed. "What on earth are you doing here in Amsterdam? You are supposed to be in prison." So I told her that I was just released and was trying to get home to Zaandam.

She handed me a piece of Swedish white bread that the Red Cross had sent to Holland. I ate it slowly and loved it very much. Then she gave me a ride on the back of her bike, and we bumped along on her bicycle with wooden wheels. After several hours and about thirty miles, we finally arrived home.

—◇—

My family smiled a lot and cried a little, but did not say too much. They were exhausted after the long years of war and after the intensely cold "hunger winter," struggling every day to survive.

Through a good friend they received some rice, which I was to eat very slowly to regain some strength after the prison food. Also, a good bath when some water came out of the faucet—which happened once a week—and a fine comb to help get rid of the lice.

A couple of days later I felt quite refreshed and climbed on my bike to see if I could make contact with some of my Resistance friends. When I arrived in Amsterdam, I was immediately followed by two German SS officers on bicycles. I then realized that it would be much wiser not to get involved so as not to endanger other people, and I went home feeling empty. Soon after

I ran into Brinkie, van Tuyl's assistant. Brinkie had survived.

We cycled to Amsterdam together and he told me that my boss, van Tuyl, had been shot in the beginning of February. The Germans had indeed been trying to find him for four long years.[12]

38

The Celebration of Peace

On May 5, 1945, the Armistice papers were signed between the High Commands of the Allied conquerors and the defeated German High Commands.

Great celebrations were about to begin. We found a prime viewing spot on the fourth floor of an office building (where illegal meetings sometimes had taken place) overlooking the huge plaza in front of the Royal Castle. The plaza was crowded with people, full of anticipation. As the orange royal flag slowly rose to the top of the castle, everyone stated to smile and wave and to shout with delight. Then shots were heard coming from a building to the left of the castle. Many shots . . . machine-gun shots. Some German soldiers had been hiding in the building and, unable to accept the German defeat, used their machine guns to mow down Dutch men, women, and children. People started to run; many fell down, dead. Some tried to find shelter behind the street organs set up to play music to celebrate the beginning of freedom. We watched in horror, unable to believe what we had just seen. Then there was silence.

Five minutes later, an open car full of German officers drove along the plaza. Again shots were fired, but from a different direction now. The officers slumped forward, killed by Resistance workers.

The dead and wounded were carried away. The plaza began to fill again with men, women, and children. After another five minutes the big parade of the Allied Forces began. And the celebrations started.

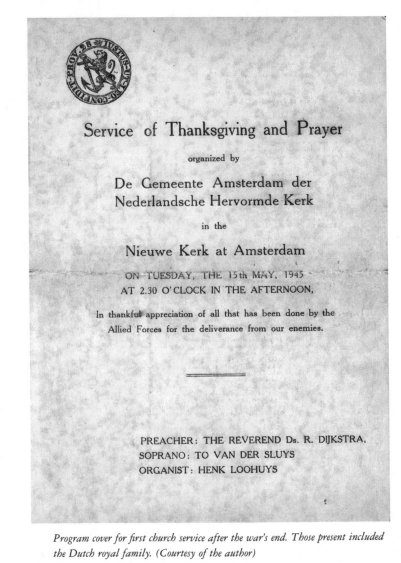

Service of Thanksgiving and Prayer

organized by

De Gemeente Amsterdam der Nederlandsche Hervormde Kerk

in the

Nieuwe Kerk at Amsterdam

ON TUESDAY, THE 15th MAY, 1945
AT 2.30 O'CLOCK IN THE AFTERNOON,

In thankful appreciation of all that has been done by the
Allied Forces for the deliverance from our enemies.

PREACHER: THE REVEREND Ds. R. DIJKSTRA,
SOPRANO: TO VAN DER SLUYS
ORGANIST: HENK LOOHUYS

Program cover for first church service after the war's end. Those present included the Dutch royal family. (Courtesy of the author)

The scene in the square in front of the Royal Castle on Armistice Day, May 5, 1945. These photographs were taken by my friend Brinkie. (Courtesy of the author)

39

THE THREE RIVERS

The three rivers are still flowing from the east through the flat lands of Holland, until they reach the North Sea.

The longboats are moving again, silent and steadfast, representing a land that suffered and survived.

Epilogue

ARNHEM, 1945

When the war ended, a small group of us (mostly old Girl Scout friends) banded together to travel to the villages surrounding Arnhem to dig out and clean homes so they could be inhabited

The ruins of Arnhem, 1945. (Courtesy of the author)

Me and two friends in June 1945. I am in my cleaning outfit, before leaving for Arnhem.

again. We worked hard for many hours during those days, but in the later part of the afternoons we spent time wandering around in the forests.

There was silence under the tall and dark trees; the crowns of the trees touched and formed a cathedral to guard the moss-covered grounds where many signs of the 1944 battle still remained.

We found uniform patches, medals, and, occasionally, a red beret from the British Airborne Division. I even found a small sketchbook that had belonged to a soldier who must have perished there.

A large cemetery was built outside of Arnhem where hundreds upon hundreds of graves were dug. Each grave had a

A group of us on the way to Arnhem to clean up houses in June 1945. I am standing and wearing a white dress. (Courtesy of the author)

A break during our work in Arnhem, June 1945. We are cooling off in the Rhine River. I am wading at the right. (Courtesy of the author)

white gravestone on top. Rows of those white gravestones are still there, as a silent army in formation reminding us of what happened there in the early fall of 1944.

Uniform patches I found in the woods surrounding Arnhem in June 1945. (Courtesy of the author)

*Sketches from a soldier's sketchbook I found near
Arnhem in June 1945. (Courtesy of the author)*

TAR AND FEATHERS

Many times the people who had fought and lost friends and family members in their battle against the oppressors took the law into their own hands. They took the people who had collaborated with the enemy in one way or another and shaved their heads, put brown burlap sacks on them, and covered them with tar and feathers. They put them on farm wagons with wooden wheels and paraded them through the streets. The hungry crowd watched, screaming and yelling with disgust and shouting out obscenities at the prisoners. The whole scene was barbaric and medieval, but I enjoyed it as much as all the others watching.

Thinking back about those events, I realize how hard we all had become, how the war had turned us into tough and cold creatures.

The Concentration Camp

The traitors during the war were now interned in concentration camps in Holland. I must admit that those camps seemed luxurious compared to the concentration camps in Germany. Treatment was excellent, as was the food. I know, because in my next job I became, with two other women, a leader of a female concentration camp.

I felt high and mighty in a Dutch Army uniform with a big *parabellum* ("pistol") hanging from my hip. The prisoners fought a lot, partially due to boredom, I am sure, and we had to break up fights often.

The Dutch Navy men stationed close by became our friends and taught us sharpshooting, so we still "played" war for a short time longer in this camp. Fortunately, the prisoners did not hate us too much, and occasionally I was presented with a beautiful sweater knitted by an inmate.

Sometimes we had to guard and transport a pregnant woman, due to deliver, to a hospital in a nearby town. After the birth, they were transported back to the camp, where inmates were delighted to help care for the new mother and child.

All were awaiting trials and, in general, received very light sentences. It did not take me very long to become restless in this strange job, and I left after three months to become employed in the castle of her majesty, Queen Wilhelmina.

A GOOD FRIEND

Queen Wilhelmina of the Netherlands had escaped with her family to England in the beginning of World War II and eventually moved to Canada.

When peace finally came in 1945, she returned to her country and donated half of her palace, Het Loo, to the people who had been in prisons and concentration camps and who needed some time for rest and relaxation. This half was renovated for this purpose and I, by now twenty years old, became a "cheer-up nurse" to the patients. My job was to help everyone there have a good time.

Every night the queen came to have tea with us in the tearoom, and the high and mighty monarch really became our very good friend indeed.

One day I was walking in the beautiful park belonging to the queen's palace. On my shoulder leaned a young man who had lost a leg in a concentration camp during the war. We walked slowly. Far in the distance I noticed a person on a bicycle. When the person came closer, I recognized her—it was her majesty, the queen.

The queen stepped off her bike, and I asked, "Does your majesty wish for me to hold your bike?" A big mistake, because if the queen wants something, she will tell you. So, bike in hand, the queen started to walk with us along the pathways of her park.

The Palais Het Loo, Queen Wilhelmina's castle in Apeldoorn. (Courtesy of the author)

A long distance from us was a gardener at work, and suddenly the queen hollered, "You can get up now. *I* am coming!"

The gardener jumped up and started bowing, and he bowed and he bowed until we were past him. Then the queen turned around and said to him, "Now you can go back to work," and she continued her very casual conversation with us as if nothing had happened.

STICHTING HERSTELLINGSOORDEN VOOR OUD-ILLEGALE WERKERS

Paleis Het Loo
Apeldoorn

Identiteitskaart

In bovengenoemd herstellingsoord is op

1 Febr. 194*6*

medewerker
als patiënt(e) opgenomen

Mej. D. H. Eikema

DE ADMINISTRATEUR.

P. DE RIDDER

Het lopen en liggen op de grasvelden in het Koninklijk Park is verboden. Er mogen geen bloemen worden geplukt en vuil mag niet in het park worden achtergelaten. Men dient zich te houden aan de aanwijzing van toezichthoudend personeel.

My Het Loo identity card. (Courtesy of the author)

FEELINGS

So often I hear the question, "How did you feel during the war, when you were in prison, when you were hungry, when you had such responsibilities in the Resistance?"

Let me try to explain the difference between then and now, the difference between wartime and peacetime.

We in Holland never talked much to each other about feelings. It's not that we did not have feelings, we simply kept them to ourselves. The Dutch people were and are, in general, quite stoic. I am often asked if I was afraid while in prison. Of course I was afraid, of course I thought of dying, but those thoughts I brushed aside. There were other things we had to deal with first and foremost, such as the daily survival of ourselves and others; such as the outsmarting of the enemy, which became our sport.

Nothing that is normal in peacetime is normal in war, but all the horrible happenings during wartime become normal eventually.

WHY

When we first became active Resistance workers, we were law-abiding citizens trying to help those who needed help. But as it became harder to help, we became less law-abiding. When I needed a better bicycle to enable me to help the Jewish people more efficiently, I immediately was provided a better bicycle, a "liberated" (stolen) one. When anything was badly needed, it was simply stolen—always from somebody who was unsympathetic to the "cause," the cause to resist the occupational forces, the cause to fight for freedom. But it was stolen, nonetheless!

The same happened when certain Germans had to be killed because they were considered dangerous to the Resistance. The simple solution was to kill them. It was a killing for the good cause. But it was murder, nonetheless!

It is very hard to go back to being a normal, law-abiding citizen after having been involved and having participated in smaller and larger crimes during a war, even when the rationale was "all for the good cause."

HEADING FOR SWEDEN

When the war was over, I was approached to participate in an organization that helped to bring surviving Jewish people to Israel by traveling secretly through Europe (The Exodus). For this purpose a reference was written by Mr. Buys. I thought about this new "job" a long time, but I desperately wanted to get away from it all, away from the people who could not forget, and away from memories, away to see a different land. So I boarded a small ship in Rotterdam on a foggy fall day, waved good-bye to my family, and headed for Sweden and ultimately the United States.

Jb Buijs
12 Rembrandtstraat
Zaandam
                                        Zaandam,9Jun.'45

This is to certify that Miss EIKEMA, A.H. has assisted
in the work of the N.S.F. since September 1944.
In the middle of August 1944 she asked me, if she could be
used in the N.S.F. Before availing ourselves of her ser-
vices, we have of course made inquires about her.
These inquires proved that she has worked for Jews and so-
called "divers" for a year and that she was giving exellent
satisfaction.
After she had joined the N.S.F. she soon proved to be such
a valuable member that she was entrusted with the most difficult courier-work etc.
Wing to her having a retentive memory and being rather en-
terprising, she succeeded in everything she undertook.
Unfortunately she was arrested towards the end of January
together with Mr W. van HALL. She was in the AMSTELVEENSCHE-
WEG Prison for three months and then too, she proved to be
very plucky. Nothwithstanding the cumming interrogations she
has betrayed nothing, in consequence of which it has also
been possible that the N.S.F. could go on with its task.

                                        Signed,

                                        Jb. Buijs.

                        Member of the managing Commitee of the
                                                        N.S.F.

My reference letter for participation in travel through Europe. (Courtesy of the author)

Montana, 1996

I remember many faces, young ones and old, white faces with large worried eyes. I remember that sometimes there were tears in those eyes and the mouths were trembling. I remember a shy smile on some of those faces, but never a broad, happy smile.

Sometimes in the early mornings the fog is thick and blankets all that is around us. We move slowly and carefully and are somewhat tense. Then the fog rises, tree trunks become taller, and suddenly the sun peeks through. The fog has lifted, the trees and the mountains and the sky are here—all at once. The world is reborn, alive again, and the sun shines brightly in the ever larger sky.

Notes

1. (*page 3*): The *Hindenburg* was an airship, or zeppelin, similar to a blimp but with a rigid inner frame, launched by Germany in 1936. It made several successful flights, even carrying passengers across the Atlantic, but was destroyed in 1937 in a fire that killed thirty-six people.

2. (*page 5*): "In Holland Stands a House," a traditional children's song translated from Dutch. As children, we sang this and many other songs in our classes.

3. (*page 11*): An *aak* (plural *aken*) is a boat that navigates by itself, but can also be combined with up to six others and pushed as barges by a tugboat.

4. (*page 34*): *As You Like It*, William Shakespeare, act 2, scene 7, line 140.

5. (*page 68*): After the war ended, we were delighted to finally see English and American movies again. One of my favorites was *The Scarlet Pimpernel*. The main character, played by Leslie Howard, reminded me so very much of the tall, charming gentleman from the Friday morning meetings.

6. (*page 81*): This quotation is from a speech Winston Churchill, Prime Minister of Great Britain, gave before the House of Commons on June 4, 1940.

7. (*page 87*): This was the first part of a poem written in Dutch in 1941 by Jan R. Th. Campert, who was later shot to death. I found the poem in a small book of illegal poems called *Poems of the Resistance*, which was given to me after the war. The poems were selected by K. van Boeschoten and Dr. L. J. Zimmerman. The first public edition appeared in November, 1945, and was printed by the printing company Albedon in The Hague, under the direction of N.G. van der A. and published with the cooperation of the publishing company De Telg in Amsterdam.

8. (*page 91*): "Why Don't You Go and Work" and *"Le jour et la nuit"* ("The Day and the Night") were songs that we sang in high school in our French and English classes.

9. (*page 92*): "Taps." We learned the Dutch words to this song, often played at military funerals in the United States, in Girl Scouts.

10. (*page 96*): That particular night, when we were to be transported to a concentration camp in Germany, the Allied forces had closed off the border between Holland and Germany, so transportation of political prisoners was impossible from then on. The underground sabotage groups who had heard about this possible transportation had planned a coup to rescue us, but were refused permission by the commander of the underground forces, as too many lives could have been lost.

11. (*page 99*): This letter from my father to our relatives in northeastern Holland was written on February 10, 1945. Names were abbreviated for safety's sake. The family lived three hours away by train or car.

12. (*page 114*): The Friday morning meeting where we were arrested had been reported to the Germans by a Resistance worker who, unbeknowst to his wife, had a mistress. The mistress had been arrested two days earlier, and the Resistance worker went to the Germans to save her by telling them about the upcoming Friday morning meeting. The other four members of my group were also executed by the Germans. My sentence was life in prison. The Resistance worker, who had betrayed us, was killed by the Resistance forces.

Acknowledgments

So many friends I must thank. First and foremost, my dearest friends from my writers' group: Peggy Christian, Jeanette Ingold, Wendy Norgaard, and Dorothy Hinshaw Patent, who worked incredibly hard and long to help me remember and constantly asked for more stories and who taught me how to put it on paper.

There are Cathi Darrington and Rita Norton, who typed and retyped for me and, as magicians, put it on computer.

And there is Les, my man, who has more patience than anybody I have ever met and who encouraged me constantly to keep writing.

I thank my brother-in-law, Jan Meyer, in Holland, who always gave me the correct information on details and who researched and found answers on facts I did not remember after fifty years.

My editor, Virginia Duncan, who in her very kind and gracious way never tired of asking me to paint the picture instead of just tell my story, deserves my sincere appreciation.

And thanks to my son, Jan Rappe, who urged me to write this story down; my daughters, Olleke Rappe-Daniels, Hedvig Rappe-Flowers, and Liedeke Rappe, for their unwavering support and trust; and my granddaughter Erika Flowers, who keeps asking me, "Grandmother, tell me about when you were a little girl and when you were in a war."

Finally, I want to thank, with all my heart, Bill Yates, who wrote a letter to me from which I quote: "Thank you for reading the introduction to your new book, *Sky*. It brought back very emotional memories for me, memories that I have not felt since I was a five-year-old. It suddenly made me realize how complacent I have become, and how important it is to remember the past. Funny how a few words can transport one back to a starless night, secure on the shoulders of a father whose stride never faltered, despite the total blackness and the dancing lights (in London, England, during WWII). Thank you for reminding me that everyone who remembers should ensure that no one forgets."

Hanneke Ippisch
Montana

Suggested Reading

Fiction

Lowery, Lois. *Number the Stars*. Boston: Houghton Mifflin, 1989 and New York: Dell, 1992.

Matas, Carol. *Lisa's War*. New York: Atheneum, 1989.

Matas, Carol. *Code Name Kris*. New York: Atheneum, 1990.

Reuter, Bjarne. *The Boys from St. Petri*. New York: Dutton Children's Books, 1994.

Van Stockum, Hilda. *The Winged Watchman*. Bethlehem, Washington: Bethlehem Books, 1996.

Vos, Ida. *Anna is Still Here*. Boston: Houghton Mifflin, 1993 and New York: Puffin Books, 1995.

Vos, Ida. *Hide and Seek*. Boston: Houghton Mifflin, 1991 and New York: Puffin Books, 1995.

Nonfiction

Bachrach, Susan D. *Tell Them We Remember: The Story of the Holocaust*. Boston: Little Brown, 1994.

Friedman, Ina. *The Other Victims: First-Person Stories of Non-Jews Persecuted by the Nazis*. Boston: Houghton Mifflin, 1990.

Greenfeld, Howard. *The Hidden Children*. Boston: Houghton Mifflin, 1993.

Meltzer, Milton. *Rescue: The Story of How Gentiles Saved Jews in the Holocaust*. New York: HarperCollins Children's Books, 1991.

van der Rol, Ruud and Rian Verhoeven. *Anne Frank—Beyond the Diary: A Photographic Remembrance*. New York: Viking, 1993.

Memoirs

Auerbacher, Inge. *I Am a Star: Child of the Holocaust*. New York: Prentice Hall, 1987.

Deschamps, Helene. *Spyglass*. New York: Henry Holt, 1995.

Frank, Anne. *Anne Frank: The Diary of a Young Girl*. New York: Bantam, Doubleday, Dell, 1988.

Roth-Hano, Renee. *Touch Wood: A Girlhood in Occupied France*. New York: Simon & Schuster Books for Young Readers, 1988; Puffin Books, 1989.

Sender, Ruth M. *The Cage*. New York: Simon & Schuster Books for Young Readers, 1986.

Weisel, Elie. *Night*. New York: Bantam, 1982.

INDEX